St angers Corner

Mary Hope Williams

068898758

LOLLIPOP MEDIA LTD.
21 DENMARK RD WIMBLEDON
London SW19 4PG

Strangers Corner
Copyright © Mary Hope Williams

ISBN 0-9538421-0-X

Published by LOLLIPOP MEDIA LTD.

Designed & Produced by Off The Wall Associates

Printed in Great Britain

Strangers Corner

DEDICATION

TO THE FAMILY

Family Relationships 1975

Frank m Margaret

Arthur m Penelope 1888 — Fanny — Ada

Minnie m Francis 1886 — Arthur m Martha

Harold

Mollie m Herbert (Ned)

Francis m Constance
- Francis m Joan
  - Hugh
  - Miranda

Harold m Sheila
- Joanna
- Sarah
- Matthew

Mary m David
- Anne
- Paul

Anne m Jan
- Katherine
- Elizabeth
- Tony
- Mark

John m Madeline
- Henry
- Arthur
- Mary
- William
- Ruth

Ruth m Peter
- Mark
- Eleanor
- Phyllida
- Timothy
- Francis

Sylvia m John
- Roderick
- Richard
- Penelope
- Ben

Anthea m Ralph
- Cecillia
- Peter
- Tessa
- Stephen
- Timothy
- James

Contents

Contents

Preface and Acknowledgements

This is a true story of a family, real events that have been remembered and recorded, the information checked whenever possible against written public documents such as birth and death certificates and army records, and personal records such as letters. Because of the disruption caused by two World Wars some records have inevitably been lost, although the events described are near enough in time to be able to rely on some personal reminiscences for their authenticity. Some unusual locations and buildings. such as Lorton Hall in Cumbria and the convent at Mons in Belgium, have been visited and explored. Historical events are portrayed as seen through the eyes of members of the family as they experienced them.

However within a family circle each member of it will have had different recollections concerning what they may consider important, or on the other hand have no recollection of events others may have personally experienced as important or traumatic. No historian can be sure that a definitive record of past events has ever been produced if they have only written records to rely upon. No biographer can be certain that they have obtained the whole truth concerning their subject and anyone who writes an autobiography is likely to leave out events it would be unwise to admit to. But within the limitations imposed by personal experience, this is an attempt to tell the true story of an ordinary, or perhaps not quite so ordinary family.

Mary Hope Williams
Oxfordshire, September 2000

Chapter One
Something To Celebrate

All her life, Mollie thought, as she lay awake in bed this morning, she had wanted to be ordinary - conventional even, but all her life extraordinary happenings interfered with this half-felt wish. Besides she had to admit that everyday life tended to bore her to distraction.

Whenever she settled down to some kind of humdrum existence, she began to feel restless, she wanted to change things, to move on, to make life more interesting and amusing. Now unbelievably it was June, 1975, and the day of her diamond wedding celebrations. She got out of bed and walked over to the window to be greeted by bright sunshine and a glorious blue sky. It was just as well it would be fine, for the children had insisted on arranging a party. There just below the window she idly watched the dancing shadows of the leaves on the hazel tree outside. She heard her old cock crowing in the hen run, listened to the chorus of early morning bird song, and admired the bright plumage of the woodpecker foraging on the lawn. Living here in this house had always given her great satisfaction. After a while she got back into bed and lay watching Ned beside her as he snored in his sleep, with his white tousled hair just visible above the bedclothes. Had they really been married for all those years? It was hard to believe they had grown so old in each other's company, had such a struggle to survive, had such exciting times.

Celebrations began as early as breakfast time. There was a timid knock on the bedroom door, and Timmy, one of her many grandsons appeared in the doorway.

"I've brought you breakfast in bed," he said, advancing with a tray which Mollie perched precariously on her knees as she took it from him. "There's all these," he continued placing an armful of cards on top of Ned, "and this - Mum said specially to show you this." Ned struggled to sit up, cards tumbling round him, as he took the proffered envelope.

"A telegram of congratulation from the Queen, no less," he announced proudly. Proof that this was a very special day, a public recognition of those long eventful years they had spent together.

"You can't not have a party," the children said. "Everyone that has been married that long deserves a party. We'll arrange it all, you won't have to worry about a thing." And although the house seemed full of the family for the last few days, arriving, departing, furtively carrying things about, moving furniture, whispering in corners, they managed somehow not to create too much of a disturbance in organising it.

So now here they were, she and Ned, sitting on deck chairs on the freshly mown lawn, visitors milling around them in droves. Ned still seemed sleepy, he often did these days. He appeared to have something on his mind too, she didn't like to see that bothered look on his face. She tried once or twice to find out what it was all about, but Ned wouldn't say. She determinedly dismissed any such worries from her mind. Today they would concentrate on this special occasion.

At that moment there was a great commotion as an indignant hen flew squawking across the grass, followed by a horde of children of diverse ages, running after it with whoops and cat calls, obviously enjoying the chase. They scattered guests in all directions as they tried to corner the straying bird. Poor thing, thought Molie, how had it got out? Too bad, it was being frightened to death. Fortunately peace was soon restored as the bird was recaptured and returned to the chicken run.

"Children have far too much freedom these days, don't you think? One of those little boys nearly knocked me over as he ran past me, such manners, so rude of him not to look where he was going," complained an elderly spinster cousin, one of the guests who was walking by. "People don't seem to know how to bring up children these days, do they?"

"Oh do you think so?" Mollie said mildly. "I hope you weren't hurt."

"That's not the point," the cousin said, still aggrieved. It was a strange fact of life that people without children usually thought they knew best how to bring them up. Mollie's own seven children would never have fallen out of trees, been rescued from drowning, ridden spirited horses, got lost on those long rambling walks they so much enjoyed, had she not been able to allow them as much freedom as they wanted. Mothers, she thought, should always know when something might be wrong, and be there only when they knew they were really needed. Extra-sensory perception she thought they called it nowadays. Children should be allowed to experiment with their lives.

"Useless, useless," she muttered to herself, as she looked down at the hands in her lap. They were somewhat gnarled and misshapen with rheumatism and she had to admit they tended to shake nowadays which made her clumsy. She was quite glad to have such a legitimate excuse for not doing anything to help today, and could just sit there enjoying the garden. The noise of all those people was like listening to the sounds of sea tides murmuring in the distance, as they washed in and out on the shore.

"Thank you, thank you, very kind of you," she and Ned repeated as they acknowledged yet another provider of yet another parcel as it landed on Mollie's lap. She attempted rather inefficiently to open it, so Ned did it for her.

"What a very pretty jug." she said enthusiastically. But all these presents, it was getting rather embarrassing, at their age they had all they needed, and where was she going to put everything? It was kind of people, very thoughtful, but she didn't like to think of them wasting their money like this.

She looked across the grass to where those seven children of hers were standing in an untidy row to have a photograph taken. It was a long time since they had all been together, and a long way for some of them to have come - from Canada for instance. Who would recognise these prosperous middle class parents standing there, some of them grandparents too for that matter, who had once been those lively difficult children she had such a struggle to bring up. They came and stood behind the deck chairs, more photos were taken, and then they drifted away again.

An irate figure with a stick advanced towards her - a red face, moustache, blue blazer - and then she saw who it was - the retired colonel who had recently moved into the house along the lane.

"They've cut the wire," he said, brandishing his stick in a menacing kind of way. Mollie was nonplussed.

"What wire?" She looked round helplessly.

"How dare you threaten my wife like that," Ned said indignantly, half struggling out of his deck chair. John, her youngest son, joined in the altercation.

"Then why did you block the right of way?" he demanded.

"It's my land, I have every right to keep out trespassers."

"That path along the river bank has been used by the villagers for hundreds of years."

"River be damned, it's nothing but a little stream. I'll take you all to court for this, see if I don't?"

"You wouldn't dare, you would lose anyway. We have a copy of the deeds of the land adjoining the river - it's called the river Hart for your information - and the right of way is clearly marked on it."

So that was what all that coming and going had been about last night, someone had been down there cutting through the recently erected wire fence next door. John had always been belligerent about rights of way, and as usual he had taken the law into his own hands she supposed. Good for him, she thought.

"How ever many times you put up that fence we will only cut it down again," was John's parting remark as the colonel retreated, shaking his fist.

Mollie wasn't seeing all that well today, the sun seemed to be in her eyes. She adjusted the spectacles that were forever falling off the end of her nose. She was trying to identify some more of the faces among the guests strolling across the lawn - cousins, friends, in-laws, all chatting together animatedly. What a lot they all seemed to have to say to one another.

Of course there was that one face above all others she would have liked to see, but she knew already he wouldn't be there. Not that she had any idea what he might look like. But she would recognise him just the same, she was sure of it, you would always know a thing like that, wouldn't you?

Ned glanced at his wife sitting there beside him, small and

freckled. Her hair was still identifiable as having once been red but it was now flecked, neither grey nor red nor white, as if pepper and salt had been carelessly sprinkled over her head. Her faded blue eyes could still have a sharp look in them sometimes, despite a somewhat bewildered expression on her face he had lately come to recognise. He wished he could have made it possible for her to have her greatest wish fulfilled this very day. It would have made a wonderful climax to the diamond wedding celebrations for her. On the other hand perhaps it was just as well it had not been possible to arrange it, since it might have made it rather awkward for everyone else who was here. He hoped something could be arranged later.

He wiped his handkerchief across his forehead, it was getting much too hot sitting here in the sun. He wished he had the energy to move to a shadier place. A fly settled irritatingly on his nose, he tried to swat it with his hand but it kept coming back.

Mollie, as she looked at all those bright splashes of colour moving over the green grass, thought of some words Ned was fond of quoting, something to the effect that:

Middle age ends, and senescence begins,
When your children and family outnumber your friends.

She idly started counting family numbers - seven children with their seven spouses - well over twenty grandchildren - their number was continually being added to - several great grandchildren running around somewhere or other - then she lost count.

She looked over at the diamond wedding cake standing on a table close by. She couldn't see the decorations on the cake clearly from where she sat but she had been told that the cake had seven separate panels, each one decorated like a family tree, with girls as pink circles, boys as blue, and an initial in the centre of each. She quite liked that idea, she could have a look later and sort them all out in her mind.

Ruth came and glanced at her parents sitting there together - her father joking with one of the guests, her mother with that rather blank expression on her face that she had noticed lately. Rather a sad face, she thought, surrounded by those wisps of peppery grey hair, some tinted reddish brown from her constant cigarette smoking. Mollie had smoked since the terrible days of the First World War, and it didn't seem kind to stop her now. Very dangerous though, Ruth thought to herself disapprovingly, she will set herself alight one of these days. She was always acutely aware of the dangers and problems of old age - after all she worked in a small local hospital with many ageing patients in her care. She brought her parents a welcome cup of tea.

"You are still by far the best looking of my children." Mollie said, but not so that anyone could hear. Ruth had been the prettiest of her children, and the fact that her daughter now lived next door she found a comfort. She was familiar and reliable - a trained nurse, though that made her seem very bossy at times. Ruth helped her parents to their feet, and the chairs were moved into the shade, where they could both relax in greater comfort. It really was a very hot day. People started drifting past again to congratulate them, among them Ned's two maiden sisters.

"Who would have thought you would produce such a large family? Father and mother would have been astonished to see them all," said the older one.

"You must be very proud of them, Herbert," said the younger one.

"I suppose so," said Mollie in a slightly off-hand way. How did one answer a stupid remark like that. They had always been so critical in the past, those sisters of Ned, she hoped they were not being sarcastic now. They didn't really approve of large families these days, she knew that. Were they also hinting that her children had not prospered as well as they might? Of course there was always something to worry about regarding one's children, but after all they seemed to have managed to look after themselves pretty well over the years. Difficulties had cropped up every now and again, they always did in families. They had got themselves good jobs, hadn't they? They had all got married, hadn't they? But none of them turned out exactly as she imagined they would.

'Tinker, Tailor, Soldier' - well they had all been in the services - caught up in the Second World War - a soldier in Burma, an army nurse in the Middle East, a VAD at that terrible Belsen concentration camp, a Wren in the Navy at Portsmouth, an RAMC doctor in Germany. Even the youngest - the twins - had been in action, as it were, machine-gunned by a passing German plane as it flew low past their upstairs classroom windows one day.

"The pilot was flying so low we could see him staring at us from the cockpit, and then he opened fire as we flung ourselves on the floor. Why would he want to shoot school children?" they asked indignantly.

They had done other things since, of course - accountant, lecturer, poet, paediatrician, nurse, horse breeder, nurse - that was the tally, not so bad when you came to think of it.

Why did those two sisters of Ned have to sound so condescending? Why did they persist in calling him Herbert? She had never liked her husband's first name, it didn't suit him a bit, it had such a hollow kind of sound, so demeaning somehow. But Ned - since Edward was his second name - seemed to suit him very well, so why couldn't they call him that as she did? Those hats - Mollie never wore a hat herself - they still wear those feathery hats, she thought, as the two sisters faded into the background again, much to her relief.

Her spinster sisters-in-law had always been quite kind, but she could never feel at ease with them since she discovered how horrible they were to Ned when they were children together. Anyway, she felt they disapproved of her, the whole of their family had never wanted Ned to marry her in the first place. Poor Ned. It seemed he was always the odd one out at home, thought of as a dunce, as a convenient cleaner of shoes and sweeper of paths, as someone to summon when jobs around the house needed to be done. His father, Ned said, always insisted that the boys of the family should look after the girls, and since the girls knew very well that they had his support, they felt they could be as nasty and bullying as they felt like being. She was glad they had wandered off. She tried so hard not to feel irritated by them.

"Dear me, wake up Ned" she said, shaking his arm, "don't you want to say hello to these friends of yours?" Ned made an effort, and greeted his friends from the local Masonic Lodge in the prescribed way. (Mollie looked the other way. Men were like small boys, she thought, with their secret signs and hidden language.) But Ned always felt appreciated and at home with the Masons, that organisation he joined so many years ago, and thought so commendable. He was glad to see his friends, she could see, and glad to receive the relayed good wishes from other Masons.

Ruth was offering them a rather worse for wear sandwich, curled at the edges. It was a pity it was so hot. Mollie tried to listen to their somewhat muffled conversation. She rather resented the secret way they seemed to talk to each other. What she wanted to know was would they have any news? Ned had told her they had been helping in the enquiries. But all she could overhear were details about a Lodge meeting Ned couldn't possibly go to, and a discussion about various charities to which she hoped he would not feel obliged to subscribe. She resented that too, considering how hard up she and Ned had always been. Then the two of them excused themselves, saying they had other calls to make. It was too bad of them, continually asking for money, thought Mollie.

"Have they found out anything?" she asked anxiously when they had gone, "anything at all?" Ned shook his head.

"They'll tell me if they do, no good keep pestering them," was all he would say.

It was time apparently for the grandchildren to present stories and poems and pictures they had provided in honour of the occasion. She liked the sound of their childish laughter. It was the carefree note in their voices that so pleased her.

Chapter Two
Unfamiliar Faces

She put on her glasses and she and Ned did their best to read the proffered offerings. Ned was lucky, he had to wear glasses ever since he was a child, but now he could see perfectly well without them. Mollie found it difficult to see anything at all. He read and quoted a few lines, they praised the drawings, and said they would read the rest of the poems and stories later.

More people appeared. Who were they all, these people who kept materialising like ghosts from the past? They were people she knew she ought to know - she had probably known them for years. But as she peered at them through her glasses, she couldn't think what their names were or why she knew them so well. Recent friends - at least she could remember something about them - but not these ghosts of times past. She glanced again at Ned - he, like herself, was concentrating on being polite, and keeping awake. He was even making a joke or two, enjoying the company. It was after all very kind of everyone to come. But if only they would go away again soon, she was getting so tired.

"The garden is looking very nice," someone remarked. Mollie was pleased, that was something she felt able to contribute - removing some of the weeds and letting the flowers be seen. That long herbaceous border down the middle of the garden was still attractive. She was constantly losing the trowels and garden forks, so she had taken to borrowing forks, even spoons from the kitchen instead. The proper tools were still hiding round the garden somewhere.

She always loved the look of the house, the white walls and thatched roof of the two old farm cottages now joined into one, the little river that ran along behind the garden hedge. 'Strangers

Corner' she decided to call the house when they moved in nearly thirty years ago. It had been an old family house name, the name of a Wiltshire farm of many generations back. She loved the house. The old cottages were built, Ned had taken the trouble to find out, in the sixteenth century.

"It's very old," he said, almost in awe, as if its being old was the acme of perfection. She agreed with him, for once. She hated modern houses, modern towns. This ancient house with its low ceilings, and chimneys through which you could stare up at the sky, suited her very well. There was even an ancient bread oven beside the fire which she had always wanted to use, the smell of fresh baked bread would give anyone an appetite. The narrow rather treacherous stairs at each end of the building, all the inconveniences, its somewhat dilapidated state, the uneven wooden floors, she wouldn't change a thing even if she could. None of your modern, so-called comfortable places appealed to her in the slightest. She wanted none of that unhealthy central heating, or floor carpeting. This was the house where she knew she belonged. It was the garden, the surrounding fields, the look of the house, the feel of the place too that mattered so much to her.

It was Mary who first saw the ghost. Practical, unimaginative Mary who asked why there was a strange woman in her bedroom, a woman who was standing there looking sad and who then had unaccountably disappeared. Others had seen her since, like her grandchildren when they were small. They would often refer to 'the lady' whom they said they chatted to in that same bedroom. She seemed a friendly enough ghost by all accounts, although people from the village would never go anywhere near that room. In case they came upon that very apparition, they said with apprehension. Gossip was that a woman with an illegitimate child had been concealed there, and in despair had thrown her infant out of the window. It was an uncomfortable story.

"I must go and feed the hens," she said to Ned abruptly. She suddenly felt the urge to be moving, she was getting cramp in her legs in this uncomfortable chair and she wanted to be away from the crowds. Besides, she wanted to see that the stray hen was all right.

Why anyone should think a deck chair comfortable she couldn't imagine. Ned merely said someone else was feeding the hens today, but she took no notice. Despite her light weight and small slim build she rather painfully struggled out of the deck chair, nearly falling as she did so. Then she set out to walk across the little bridge over the ditch behind the house and went into the chicken run. She felt she could breathe again. She pulled up some weeds to throw to the hens.

She examined the vegetable patch on the way back. That's another thing about living here, she thought to herself with some satisfaction. They could grow their own vegetables, and with the eggs from the hens, there was always plenty of wholesome food about. Why, for the last few years they had more or less lived off the eggs and vegetables. It was only necessary to buy meat when people came to visit. She and Ned didn't need much money now to supply their everyday needs.

She threw the hens a few more handfuls of the weeds, and then, as she was returning she came upon a small child crying in a lost kind of way, staring at a patch of Marigold flowers.

"Fairy," the child said. She was clutching a book with illustrations of flower fairies. What memories the scene conjured up in Mollie's mind, what emotions, at that moment she could almost feel herself a child again.

"What's your name?"

"Angela."

Mollie took Angela by the hand and led her back to the lawn. The ditch had water in it and it would be easy enough to fall in. They rejoined the company to find the child's mother. Mollie smiled back, she gave a little wave, as Angela was claimed and led away. She returned to her deck-chair and found everyone was waiting for her and Ned to cut the cake.

With much effort and some help they stood and cut the first slice and returned thankfully to sit down again. They were offered a glass of champagne. "Much overrated of course, sherry is much nicer," Mollie muttered under her breath. But she had another glass.

"Here's to the next twenty years," she said skittishly to the crowd in front of her, waving the glass rather precariously, with an amused expression on her face, a slight twinkle in her wrinkled eyes, and a suppressed hiccough. Ned was going to make a speech, she could see it coming. There would be some rather doubtful jokes, she knew, and I hope everyone is polite enough to laugh at them, she thought, although probably most people had heard them many times before.

When he said they had been married sixty years and it didn't seem a day too long she felt quite embarrassed, even more so when he said what a wonderful wife she had been, and how good - looking she still was. However mistaken he might be in his compliments, she knew he meant them. He had always been proud of her, one way and another, she'd always known that. But she found it very difficult to respond without seeming sentimental or waspish. Dear me, I wish he wouldn't, she thought to herself. But she was rather pleased all the same. For a moment she had a youthful expression again, her face lit up just like that of a small child, the critical tension in her eyes for a brief moment had gone.

They went - all those guests - at last. Or most of them. Some went home, some who were to stay longer went off to the local pub for a drink. Mollie, followed by her still sleepy husband, retreated inside. Ned was rather unsteady on his feet, it must be the champagne, she was still feeling a little light-headed herself.

What nonsense was it that John had been saying about Ned before he left? She was very proud of her son's eminence as a doctor, but he fussed so, he was always imagining there was something wrong with people when really they were perfectly all right. He was like all doctors, they thought they knew so much better than anyone else.

"He should see a doctor as soon as possible," John said as he left. "I don't think all this hot weather is at all good for him, there's something wrong, he needs a check up." Nonsense, Mollie thought, Ned will be perfectly all right now we are inside again out of the heat.

They sat in their comfortable arm-chairs in their little sitting room, where it was cool and quiet. The silence seemed almost unnerving, after all the hubbub. Ned was reading quietly to himself, immersed in some of the artistic contributions provided by the children. He passed them over for Mollie to look at. One had

Angela written in large irregular letters, with a picture of what looked like a fairy with wings. Mollie smiled to herself at the recollection of Angela's hand in hers.

"Listen to this," said Ned, giving her a gentle push to make sure she was awake and listening, as he read out a poem:

'Timbered beams and white walls in the summer sun,
The shadowed ghosts of past mistakes and sad occasions
Banished in the quiet air.

The cars draw up, left with a slam beyond the gates
Like burnished beetle shells discarded in life's toil
Sloughed off care.

The children eye each other, adults stare and look again.
Gestures they know, familiar, unfamiliar faces
Feelings they share.

The murmuring voices spread across the lawn
I'm from Australia, we're from Canada, I live in Brussels now.
Experiences compare.

The gentle stream in placid ripples flows,
And life runs quietly through the reeds of time
History made aware.

The trees make dappled shadows in the heat
And in the gentle shade of memories past, the guests
Contentment share.'

Mollie was thinking of the child who had felt lost at the party. Children should never be allowed to feel lost, such a choking feeling of absolute devastation and abandonment can arise from such incidents. I ought to know, Mollie thought, it had happened to her often enough.

"Time for bed," said Ned, realising how very tired they both were, even though it was still only nine o'clock. Mollie was reluctant to move, it seemed an effort for them both to get up the narrow stairs. Once in bed Mollie continued with past thoughts about her childhood, not sleeping, only half awake, reliving those far off days. Sometimes, she thought, those far off days seemed more real than the present ones. She tossed and turned in bed, listening to Ned's snores. She awoke in a cold sweat as she often had lately, after a nightmare whose content she could never recall. But she knew in some strange way that it was always the same nightmare, bringing with it feelings of uneasiness and guilt.

What a couple we are, she thought, Ned and me, both of us feeling uncomfortable about the past. Why can't we just make the most of the present. But we are inevitably what we are because of the past, she thought. At our age we are our past whether we like it or not. And sooner or later we have to come to terms with it.

★

'There are more things in heaven and earth than are dreamt of in your philosophy,' had always been one of her favourite Shakespearean quotations. Life was bewildering, because hidden experiences, hidden thoughts always seemed to be lurking just below the surface. There were many things that seemed to have no rational explanation at all.

Her waking life was no help in recalling what had happened to her before she was two and a half years old. People of course seldom do remember as far back as that in their childhood. But then parents usually provide at least some answers. 'What was I like when I was a baby?' 'How old was I when I began to walk? or talk?' These are the kind of questions to which children usually want answers.

Mollie had always been wary of asking her parents for any such information. Something happened when she was small, something that her parents never wanted to discuss. She knew that because she had once or twice asked her mother about her babyhood, only to see a cloud in her mother's eyes. She had come to accept the inevitable change of subject as an indication of her mother's distress, so persisted no further. She felt instinctively that breaking the barrier of silence would put her mother in some kind of jeopardy.

If she ever could have recalled what went on in her mind in those nightmares she so often had but never remembered, she would have known they were about herself and her elder brother Harold, when she was two and her brother two years older. She so adored her brother then. They had great fun together which very often got them into trouble. They teased their parents, tried out various tricks on them, and were generally quite a handful for their mother to manage. They called their mother Banna, from a favourite fairy story she often read to them. Their father, whom they called Baba from the same fairy story, often came home very late from work.

Nursery rhymes were the children's favourite games as the two of them romped together in their exuberant way. She and Harold would pretend to fall over when they came to 'Jack fell down, and broke his crown and Jill came tumbling after.' 'Tom, Tom, the piper's son, stole a pig and away he ran,' was another favourite game as they chased each other round the room, laughing and giggling at their own jokes. Harold was always inventing new games because he had learnt to read, and had a book with all the nursery rhymes in it. Mollie knew he was very clever. His parents would often praise him for reading so well, and they laughed at his jokes in a grown up kind of way. Mollie, when she was a small child, would have gone through hell and high water for her brother.

It was during a game of 'Jack fell down' that one afternoon she and Harold stumbled against a chair. Banna was standing on it, cleaning some shelves. There was a terrible crash, and their mother lay groaning on the floor. She and Harold cowered frightened in a corner. Help arrived as Elsie their maid came running into the room. Then there was utter confusion with people rushing about everywhere - Baba came home from work - nurses with white aprons fussed about - a doctor arrived with a stethoscope hanging round his neck. He kept shaking his head as he went on talking to Baba. No one took any notice of the two small children still cowering in a corner. In fact their mother had had a miscarriage, brought on by the heavy fall from the chair. She had been far on into a twin pregnancy, and she was ill for a very long time.

Harold and Mollie had never been told that for their mother the next two years had been dark days, mad days, dreadful days she wanted to forget, to obliterate from her mind for ever. She and Baba would never admit that her illness included a kind of madness, for to have madness in a family was a disgrace not to be contemplated. She felt for the rest of her life that the only way to remain in control was to bury the memory of that terrible time, lest those hidden feelings that had been unleashed then should take over again, leave her out of control. Madness was not a condition either of them would ever have admitted to, but in truth that was what she had always so feared, a returning madness, a situation out of control.

But the two children knew none of this, either then or later. Harold called their young childhood the taboo subject. One thing she and Harold knew for certain was that swift punishment had followed that accident. They were both of them, Mollie and Harold, immediately sent away from home - Mollie to a boarding school, because her aunt taught there, and her brother to his aunt and uncle who lived far away in the North of England somewhere. Mollie felt abandoned by everyone, including God, she remembered.

Chapter 3
Lonely As A Cloud

The nightmare retreated, and Mollie opened her eyes again in the present to find Ned lying in bed beside her. It had been a restless uncomfortable night. It was early morning at Strangers Corner. You could tell by the pink flush of the dawn as it brushed the room with its delicate light, and by the sound of the birds as they sleepily began to sing. No need to struggle to read the dial on her watch, it couldn't be more than about four o'clock. Mollie liked the early morning, it seemed so fresh each day, so calm. She got out of bed to try and shake off the feeling of panic that she always felt after one of those nightmares. She lit a cigarette. The thing to do with panic was to concentrate on the present, to imagine yourself part of the magic of an undisturbed natural world. She put on a dressing-gown and went for a walk round the garden. It was getting lighter every minute. There was silence except for those early morning birds. She could feel on her bare feet the dampness of the dew on the grass. She was rather pleased when someone had once called her mad Mollie, because she had been caught dancing out there on the grass in the early dawn. These days she could manage only a few uncertain steps.

Ruth - Mollie had always thought Ruth was rather like her own mother in the way she disapproved of things - Ruth would scold her if she knew how wet her feet had become. She looked at the dawn clouds, watched the birds drink from the little river, wandered over to the chicken run. The hens were out, how careless not to have locked them up last night. But thankfully there didn't seem to have been any foxes about. What murderers foxes were! She remembered one morning a few years ago when she found all the chickens dead with their heads bitten off. What a scene of devastation that had been. What a pity nature had to be so 'red in tooth and claw.' She shivered, early morning was quite cold even in summer.

After a while she went back to bed. It was warm next to Ned. He was snoring.

★

As she lay there, Mollie's mind drifted back to the day when she was about two, when she had been sent away to school - that was something she did vividly recall - her earliest memory. Her punishment, that was as clear as anything else Mollie could ever recollect.

"You'll be coming to stay with me for a while," her Aunt Ada said as she arrived late on that fateful evening. Aunt Ada was a figure she vaguely recognised as someone she might have seen before. A suitcase was hastily packed, and they set out. There was a dark and hurried journey, with her aunt sitting beside her in a carriage with an old black leather seat with worn brown lines on it. They travelled through what seemed like an endless night. Her aunt sat primly by her side, saying very little. Mollie would have liked to hold her hand, everything seemed so strange and frightening, but she dared not. She tried once, but her aunt moved slightly away, and she gave up the attempt, and dozed off.

When they arrived, she was taken into an enormous room full of shadows and dark corners, and lots of people with eyes staring hard at her from all directions. It was at that moment that she first knew the terror of complete panic. She retreated to the nearest shelter she could find, under a great big table, and cowered in the corner beside one of the thick brown wooden table legs. All she could see from her hiding place were a lot of pairs of neat boots below the bottom of a lot of dark coloured skirts. She tucked up her own legs under her dress trying to remain invisible, because she knew that if she came out from under the table all those pairs of eyes would be waiting to look at her again. "Come here at once Mollie," said the sharp voice of her aunt, as she retreated further into the corner, and carefully pulled her dress down further over her feet, as she tucked them up uncomfortably beneath her, hoping no one could see her.

"Shan't."

"Don't be frightened, dear," said another kindlier voice.

"Shan't." Mollie repeated.

"Do you think, Miss Winder," began the kinder voice, "that it might be better....?"

"She needs a firm hand," said her aunt's voice. "You don't know her as I do." Mollie hated her aunt from that moment.

"You naughty girl, come out at once." Fight as she might, her arm was seized and she was pulled screaming into the room.

"No,"she shrieked, "No." All those faces, all those eyes. But her struggles were to no avail. She was glad when she was dragged, still struggling, away from them all. She was scolded all the while as she was carried off to bed. She felt herself being undressed despite her struggles, and put in a big bed with cold sheets. She tried not to go to sleep, but she did.

When she woke next morning she found the bed she was in was next to that of her aunt. She saw her aunt lying there, with a cap on her head, with dark curls that protruded at the edges. She looked very untidy. Mollie began to giggle, she wasn't quite sure why, but her aunt did look so comical lying there with her unruly hair.

Not a bit like the trim aunt who had scolded her last night...

"While you are here you are to sleep in this room with me," her aunt explained, as she sat up in bed, " so that I can keep an eye on you."

"Can I go home now please?" Mollie asked politely.

"You're to stay here with me at the school for the time being," she was told firmly "until your mother is quite recovered."

"I want to go home now," she wailed. She could feel tears running down her face, tasting salt in her mouth.

"You have to stay here with me. You'll understand better when you are older," was all her aunt said.

"I want to go home."

"It would upset your mother."

Her aunt made her feel on edge with her sharp, grating voice. Now she was convinced even more than ever that she was being punished, banished from home for something she shouldn't have done.

"Where's Harold?" she asked next.

"Gone to stay with your Aunt Penelope and Uncle Arthur," she was told. Mollie had no idea who Aunt Penelope might be, but Harold must have been banished like her to some awful place he had never heard of. She was alone, that she understood, and then that feeling of panic swept over her again. She wanted to run, but there was nowhere to run to. She buried her head under the bedclothes.

"You must get dressed now," said her aunt sharply. Mollie struggled to put on her things, with a slap here and an admonishment there, until she was finally told she was fit to go downstairs. Then she had to run the gauntlet of all those eyes again, as she was taken into that huge room to have breakfast. After breakfast she was taken to an equally large classroom and told to sit still, while girls sitting in straight rows were staring at her all the time.

But that day passed, and another similar day, and then another, and more time passed, as it always does. Mollie soon got used to the routine of getting herself dressed every morning, with Aunt looking on as she struggled with buttons and shoes and other difficult articles of clothing. "You can perfectly well manage, you are not a baby anymore," she would be scolded. "Hurry up, you are being slow on purpose." Or "Do take more care, that's the second time this week you have put that on back to front."

Mollie didn't cry anymore, it was not really in her nature to cry, besides, what was the point? She got used to pretending she didn't hear or care. She just stared in front of her, waiting for Aunt to stop. But Aunt wasn't always quite so cross. Sometimes she promised Mollie treats.

"You should learn to walk like a lady with your toes turned out," Mollie was told one day, "and you shall have a little present." Mollie tried for a whole week, remembering about her feet wherever she went. It felt a bit awkward, but she managed most of the time. Why do people have to turn their toes out in that uncomfortable way she wondered?

"I can walk like a lady now with my feet turned out," she told her aunt a week later.

"You'll have to do it for a lot longer than that," she was told. And Mollie never got her present.

"Sit absolutely still for five minutes and I'll take you out for a special treat," her aunt said another time. Twice Mollie sat still for those full five minutes, but of course no treat was forthcoming. Mollie got used to that too, and stopped expecting to be rewarded for trying to please her unpredictable aunt.

Every night she was bidden to say her prayers out loud, which included the one that began,

"Our Father, which art in heaven," which she soon learned by heart, and then "make me a good girl," and "God bless Mummy and Daddy."

"God always takes care of those who ask him to," her aunt said. How Mollie prayed, oh how she prayed. "Please God make Banna come and fetch me home; please God tell Baba I don't like it here; please God make Harold come and stay with me; please God, don't let aunt be cross." For quite a while she believed God would come and rescue her, He must, but He never did.

Aunt Ada didn't approve of her calling her parents Banna and Baba. That made it even more certain to Mollie that she would never ever see them again. A prayer soon became just a form of words, her faith in God slowly waned. Her aunt did once or twice mention home, but by then Mollie had forgotten what it was like.

At meal times she would find herself sitting at that great table, with lots of large chattering girls, who seemed as grown up as the teachers. She hated their treating her as if she were some kind of pet. She pushed them away and got scolded for being so rude. She soon learned to find her place by herself, before the great bell stopped ringing. Then the big main door would open, there would be a sudden silence, everyone would stand up, and her aunt and all the other teachers would march in. Grace would be said, chairs would scrape, there would be silence except for the sounds of spoons in porridge bowls, while the teachers talked together.

Aunt Ada was for ever buying her new clothes, and dressing her up with hair ribbons and sashes which made her feel uncomfortable. She hated having her hair brushed anyway, it was a painful process as Aunt insisted on getting out all the tangles from her long red tresses. Whenever there were visitors about, her aunt would show her off as if she were on display, which made Mollie put out her tongue at them all, or refuse to say good afternoon or do whatever else was required of her. Aunt liked nothing better than to hear the kind of remarks Mollie overheard on some of these occasions.

"Very good of Miss Winder to take so much trouble with her difficult little niece"or "Doesn't that child look sweet in that little pink dress?" or "What pretty red hair the little girl has." Aunt Ada didn't like that.

"Auburn," she would always correct the speaker - red hair seemed to her vulgar, as if there was something wrong with red hair. Mollie wished she could be someone else.

Chapter 4
Friends In Need

"Wake up, Ned." Mollie said, shaking him a little as he snored more loudly than ever. "Time to get up."

"What?, what?" he said gruffly.

"I wonder where everyone is?" she said.

"What?" he repeated. To her annoyance he still seemed half asleep. That was one thing you could say about Ned, he never had any trouble sleeping.

"I wonder what they are all doing downstairs?" she asked.

"Speak up, I can't hear you," he protested.

"Dear me, why don't you listen. I'm always telling you to listen more carefully. You don't pay enough attention," she said critically. Ned put on his dressing gown, shuffled into his worn slippers, and with his tousled hair and eyes that looked blinkingly at the morning light, started down the narrow stairs. He didn't need to put on his glasses. Triumphing over his lifelong short-sightedness made him feel a little less old and incapable. He knew Mollie wanted a report on the present situation, he was on his way down to investigate and make a cup of tea.

Mollie didn't want to get up as she was still tired. The prospect of putting on her damp dressing gown wet from the dew on the lawn and then facing the comments it would arouse, made her wary. Attempting to dress with her shaking hands seemed too much of a struggle. So she was grateful to him, as he made his uncertain way down the stairs. However, she listened with apprehension to the clatter of the tray as he slowly made his way up the narrow stairs again with only a rope bannister to hold onto. Why do men seem so clumsy? she wondered, one of these days he will drop the tray if he isn't more careful. He never pays enough attention to what he is doing.

He brought her a weak cup of milk-less and sugar-less tea, an orange which he proceeded to peel for her and some burnt toast. She didn't mind the burnt toast. Charcoal was good for indigestion so they said, and she had plenty of that these days. Managing to drink from the cup without spilling her tea was quite difficult today. Whenever she was tired the tremor in her hands got worse. Ned brought what news he could from downstairs.

"No letter in the post," he said. He felt acutely for her disappointment.

"Ruth is looking after Anne and Anthea, before they go back to Canada, and Sylvia and Mary and their children are downstairs, helping themselves to breakfast," he reported as he dressed.

"Where's my blue shirt?" he demanded in an irritated voice - he had been searching around in his inefficient way for some time looking for clean clothes to put on.

"Dear me," she answered, "won't another one do? There are at least four clean ones in that drawer."

"No, I need that one. Had you forgotten there's a meeting today of the residents' association? I must be there, it's the last one I'll go to. I told you - I'm resigning as chairman. I'll let someone else have the worry now. But I do need to look presentable." Mollie got out of bed, spilling some of the tea.

"Here it is," she said, extracting it and half throwing it at him. She was rather sorry he was resigning from the committee, it had given him something to do, something to think about besides those gloomy thoughts of his.

The shirt did make him look a bit smarter. She had to admit he looked quite distinguished. No wonder they called him the Major. Thank goodness, she thought, I can still do the washing. She didn't much like machines, never had, but the washing machine was certainly useful. Mind you she was very careful these days, after the time she caught her hand in the mechanical rollers and had to have her wedding ring cut off her injured finger. But this new machine was much easier to manage. She liked washing, and ironing and washing up, soothing occupations that required little thought. After all one couldn't just sit and do nothing all day.

Yes, she was sorry he was resigning. It was very peaceful when he was out at one of his meetings, she could enjoy being on her own for a while.

★

When she was small and had the chance she was so glad to escape from everyone at Aunt Ada's school. There was a garden to which Mollie could sometimes retreat - a big lawn surrounded by a border of shrubs. She found a secret place to hide in amongst the bushes where some rather straggly marigolds grew. It was a fairy place, she decided, especially when the sun was shining. Sunlight would be dancing through the leaves, with little shafts of speckled light beaming down like a fairy ladder. Fairyland must be like this, she thought, as she watched the flickering light, in that secret place full of those dancing shadows.

No one ever found her there, except once when a big girl peered in at her. For weeks Mollie was left in a state of terrible agitation, wondering would the big girl tell her aunt about her hiding place. But the girl never did. She was called Emily, and sometimes played with Mollie, or read her stories about fairies. She never came back to look at Mollie's hiding place. Emily was nice.

One day in her secret hiding place Mollie actually found a fairy. She liked those picture books of fairies, dancing or flying about amongst the flowers, but she never expected to see one. It was on a bright sunny day when green leaves were singing in the wind, and the shadows dancing, when she first saw her - sitting on a small branch as it swayed up and down in the breeze.

To and fro, up and down, it was like a fairy swing. She watched the restless quiver of the leaves as they made those little curtsies in the wind. The fairy was a bit like a gossamer dandelion seed. She had silvery wings, and an orange wand in her hand.

"Hello, who are you?" Mollie asked.

"Fairy Marigold. Who are you?"

"Mollie. Do you live here?"

"Yes, of course. But what are you doing here?"

"Hiding. I hate" - she was going to say Aunt, but she changed it to Miss Winder. "I hate Miss Winder." She thought the fairy was more likely to know who she meant if she used her Aunt's proper title.

"Come now," said the fairy, "she's not as horrid as all that, is she?"

"Worse," Mollie confided. "She stole me away from home, and she won't let me go back and she's very cross because I made my new dress dirty."

After that first day when she had met Marigold, she often talked to her. She would find her in the hiding-place sitting on a flower, or swinging on a branch. Marigold even flew into her bedroom one night when she was trying not to cry, but Mollie quickly chased her away in case her aunt found her there.

Mollie talked to her for as long as she dared. It was worth being scolded afterwards, just to stay and talk to her very own fairy. No one knew about Marigold of course. Whenever Mollie heard anyone coming close, she told Marigold to fly away, just in case.

"I really believe in fairies, don't you?" her friend Emily said one day, after they had been reading one of the fairy stories together. Mollie said nothing, just stared uncomfortably. Someone might discover Marigold if she said yes, and then she might fly away for ever. If she said no Marigold might disappear for ever anyway because Mollie had pretended she was not real.

Mollie had another friend, one of the teachers, who played music. Mollie sometimes listened outside the music room door, soft music, music you could get lost in, the kind of music that made you feel happy. Miss Jones played such lovely soft music. One day Mollie sneaked into the music room when no one else was there, and tried to play the piano for herself. It didn't sound a bit like the music Miss Jones played. She tried the tunes of some nursery rhymes she remembered, and sometimes they came out right. She was enjoying herself one day, forgetting where she was, trying one tune after another, when she was suddenly aware that Miss Jones was standing behind her. She jumped down off the stool, and tried to run away.

"Don't mind me," said Miss Jones, "I was just enjoying listening to your music. Why don't we play together." She helped Mollie to find one or two different notes when the tune didn't come out the way it should. Mollie forgot everything that afternoon except the music, she was there for quite a long time. Then of course she heard her aunt calling her, and she had to stop enjoying herself.

She never knew quite how it came about, but she found herself having music lessons everyday with Miss Jones. Playing music was second best to talking to Marigold. Third best was reading, and sometimes she hid a book after a lesson and took it to read to Marigold, and brought it back next day. She got caught once taking a book, and Aunt was very cross. Stealing she called it.

Mollie nearly decided not to play music anymore, when Aunt started interfering, making her play the pieces she had learnt in front of the whole school, or sometimes even in front of visiting parents.

"If you want me to go on paying for your music lessons, you must let me hear how well you are getting on," Aunt said. Despite hating the attention of whoever was supposed to be listening to her, all those eyes staring at her again, she really wanted those lessons very badly. So she learnt to pretend to be Miss Jones as she sat there playing, copying her mannerisms and the way she sat, the way she played. When she was pretending to be Miss Jones she didn't mind the eyes looking at her, and just played for the sake of the sounds. Pretending was a kind of protection. Sometimes she copied other teachers, Aunt included, when she was talking to Marigold. Mollie had found a way to make the best of things. Perhaps school was not so bad after all. She had got used to it

One day her aunt said she wanted Mollie to come to her teaching room after breakfast. Mollie was frightened, she had never been told to report to the study room before. It was where naughty girls had to go. Perhaps someone had found out about her hiding place. She could hardly drag her feet along to the door. Perhaps she had done something very wrong, something she knew nothing about. Or perhaps, she thought, feeling a little less frightened, there was to be a special day when she would be told to play the piano at a concert everyone had been talking about. She could hear her heart beating fast as she knocked timidly at the door.

When she was told to come in she found her aunt with a letter in her hand.

"The doctors think your mother is quite recovered now," Mollie was informed, "you're to go home this afternoon."

Mollie couldn't think whether she was pleased or sorry, she just felt bewildered. What was home, where was it, what people would be there? She would be glad to be away from her aunt, that at least she knew. Then she realised she would have to leave Marigold behind, and burst into tears. She knew fairies couldn't live anywhere too far away from near their own hiding places.

"Don't cry, dear, I thought you'd be glad to go home. Of course I shall miss you, my dear little niece, but I'll come and see you sometimes. Now give your aunt a kiss, there's a good girl, and we'll go and pack your things."

All she remembered of that journey home was the sound of the wheels, she could hear them now she thought. She woke to the sound of someone's car pulling up outside her own house and as she sat up in bed and started to listen to the various sounds she could hear in the rest of the house, she realised she must have been dreaming again. It was high time she got dressed.

Chapter 5
Unfamiliar Places

It was after she had carefully and determinedly got dressed, in easily donned trousers and top, that she negotiated the steep steps and emerged downstairs into the sitting-room. After a brief greeting to the family, she was subjected to a somewhat disjointed conversation with Mary, her eldest daughter. Mary was always organising things. She supposed anyone who had once been a nurse was like that. What had made most of her daughters nurses at one time or another, she wondered? The only one that hadn't been a nurse had chosen to look after horses instead.

"I wish Mandy was still here," Mollie said accusingly, not wanting to listen to what Mary was saying. She couldn't forgive Mary for having Mandy put down. She had been so fond of her, such a dear little dog. Somehow it was easier these days to feel close to an animal than to other human beings. Animals didn't demand anything, didn't answer back.

"You know very well," Mary said, for what to her seemed the hundredth time "there was no alternative. Mandy had kidney disease, she would have died very soon anyway and in great pain." Mollie only grunted again in disapproval.

That had been one of her reasons for wanting to live in the country. There were always animals about, rabbits and guinea pigs when the children were small, hens, cats, a pig, and most of all dogs.

"I've asked a builder to come and look at the house," Mary said hurriedly. "You never know, one or other of you may find one day that you can't manage the stairs anymore, and there is no double bedroom or bathroom down here. You would be stranded then, wouldn't you? They could convert the back kitchen."

"Nonsense, you are just trying to make things difficult. Where could we store the food? The back kitchen is the only cool place in the house. And it's very dark and damp on that side of the house anyway. We would be most uncomfortable."

"I expect the builders would need to look into that, I suspect there may be rot somewhere there. Apart from that you forget you are both well over eighty and anything could happen to either of you at any time."

"I'm not going to be made to sleep downstairs. I need to sleep upstairs. I want to keep my own room."

"You wouldn't have to move out of your room unless the need arose."

"What is the point of spending all that money then for nothing? We can't afford it anyway."

"The family would pay, of course."

"We wouldn't hear of it, would we Ned?" Mollie dug him in the ribs, he wasn't paying enough attention - couldn't he see he must put a stop to all this nonsense. Ned just grunted.

"Well, just let's see what it would cost. It might not be that much you know."

The very idea, Mollie was thinking, of being turned out of her own bed. Why was everyone always trying to upset perfectly good arrangements? Just then her favourite grandson came into the room.

"How a' ye' Grandma?" She liked the sound of his young voice.

"And what have you been up to?" she asked.

"We've all been paddling in the stream."

"Well, what do you think, Mother?" Mary was saying.

Mollie was tired of the argument, she wanted to ask Timmy about his exploration of the stream.

"I suppose so," she answered. She had forgotten what the argument was all about anyway. She just wanted to be left in peace. Everyone was always wanting to change things, it was bewildering. There had been quite enough changes in her life.

Her grandson reminded her of her own brother Harold, she enjoyed talking to him. She was glad when she was left in peace, with only Timmy there, when even Ned had departed to Ruth's house next door. Then even Timmy went.

What was it, she thought, as she sat down in her favourite old-fashioned green armchair - that used once to be her father's favourite seat - what was it in the last few days that kept taking her back to her childhood in this ridiculous way? Why did she feel so unsettled, so bothered about the long dead past? What did it really matter now? But it did. Perhaps it was because she instinctively felt things were beginning to alter once more. It was always like that, whenever things seemed to be settled, that was the point at which some new arrangement was thrust upon her.

She wouldn't admit it, even to herself, but she was beginning to worry about Ned. What if he were really ill, and she would have to manage without him? She didn't think she could survive something like that. To feel lost and betrayed once again. Just the idea brought panic to her mind. She would have to do as she always had done, prod Ned out of his present mood, push him into action. It was a question of mind over matter with him. If he thought his health would improve, then it would. She had known ever since they were first married that he needed her to help him out of these defeatist moods. No, she told herself, there was nothing really to worry about, she would make sure he was soon his old self again, even if she had to bully him into it. She would be lost without Ned.

★

She felt lost and bewildered, she remembered, with a sinking feeling of desertion, when she had been taken home again from her aunt's boarding school, after her long stay with Aunt Ada. She recollected the day she and her Aunt Ada had got into a horse bus, carrying all her belongings. She sat quietly watching the congested traffic, carts and horses and jostling people everywhere, listened to all the noise and bustle as they were driven through a street market, and out onto the more open road. Then they got a horse cab, she rather liked the comforting sounds of the horses' hooves as they trotted along the quieter roads, through rows and rows of neat houses. It seemed quite a long time before they stopped and got out and walked up the steps of a white painted house.

It was a house that seemed somehow vaguely familiar, like a

picture out of one of her fairy-story books come to life. It grew more familiar as they stood there waiting. Aunt had rung the bell. The bell sounded very loud, but there were no people about, and she began to feel confused. It was like looking at pictures in a story-book and then suddenly it was not a story but something real. Suppose she was stuck halfway between the story and what was real, suppose she would have to stand on the steps forever waiting, and no one came.

At last a maid answered. It was no one familiar. Mollie ran back down the steps afraid it was the wrong house. Aunt Ada caught her hand and held her roughly as she dragged her back up the steps and through the now open front door.

She was hugged first by a tearful lady who was standing there and then by a man whose coat smelled of wool. They both felt familiar in some vague kind of way, but not yet fully recognised.

"Welcome home, dear. My, how you have grown"! said the woman. "Let me have a proper look at my little Mollie." Mollie just felt stupefied.

"Come and give your father a kiss," the man said. His chin felt scratchy.

They hugged her and kissed her again and again which made her feel more uncomfortable. She pushed them away. She turned her back on them. They shouldn't have sent her away to school.

She was quite upset when her aunt kissed her and went, at least she had been a familiar presence in this confusing world.

"Be a good girl," she said, and just went away. Mollie's belongings were taken upstairs and she found herself standing in a strange bedroom. It had pictures of fairies on the wall; there was an old doll sitting on a chair; there were some books on a shelf. The room seemed mostly blue.

"We've had your room repainted for you," the man said.

Then she started roaming round the house, looking in every corner, as cats do in a strange place, making sure of her surroundings. She went upstairs and looked in all the other bedrooms, then down into the kitchen, and next into the little garden at the back. Everything was unfamiliar, yet somehow also strangely familiar. It was like gradually waking up after a very long dream. Objects she came across like the dresser in the kitchen, suddenly seemed to come into a different focus, like finding an old friend.

As the days passed, the strangers who had greeted her were becoming more familiar. But she ignored them still. She did as she was told, even ate her meals though she didn't feel hungry. It seemed very quiet after being used to all those chattering girls round her. She played by herself in the garden, hoping Marigold might appear, but knowing she could not really fly all that way from school. She sat on her bed reading books, found some long forgotten toys to play with, went to bed when she was told to, and dressed herself again next morning.

The maid was called Jane. Baba and Banna became familiar words again. But she didn't trust her parents - not yet. They might send her away again.

She was roaming round the house one day and found her mother cooking in the kitchen. It looked quite interesting.

"Why don't you make a jam tart for your father, he's very fond of jam tarts," Banna suggested. So she climbed up on a stool and rolled out the pastry, and when it had been cooked she gave it to Baba to eat. The pastry was rather grey looking, not white like the kind Banna had made.

"Delicious," her father said, and finished it all up.

When Baba came to sing her to sleep that night, just as he used to do, she put her arms round his neck and gave him a kiss.

"Now the day is over, night is drawing nigh," his droning voice sang.

"What does 'drawing nigh' mean?" she asked. It was explained.

As she dropped off to sleep she was thinking of a shop down the road she used to know, before she went away - Mr Knight who had a greengrocer shop whom she pictured drawing nigh with his cart - bringing apples and pears and things for her to eat next day. She felt she was home again.

She soon got used to home. It was her father however, who seemed the most familiar to her. With her mother it still seemed a little strange, something not quite comfortable, as if there was some intangible barrier between them.

Mollie missed Marigold, she missed Emily, she missed her music lessons, she missed Miss Jones. She didn't like being on her own.

"Where's Harold?" she asked some time later. She had come across one of his toys and marched around the house clutching it for days before daring to ask.

"Staying with your Uncle Arthur and Aunt Penelope."

"When will he come back here?"

"He'll come and visit us soon," Banna promised.

Banna had a new baby soon after that, a strange crumpled up pink squirming thing that was nothing like the new brother she had been told to expect. So she imagined herself a new pretend friend, a boy called Scrumpy. Scrumpy was always nice to her, he made jokes, he told her stories, he was her own special friend. The new baby was called Francis and was so tiny you had to be careful not to hurt him. He was no use to play with. He couldn't talk or anything like that. Scrumpy had a laughing face and she could have long conversations with him. She could talk to Scrumpy when she was alone in her room. He lived on her bed.

"We've got a special treat for you, Harold is coming to stay next week," Banna informed her one day. "I expect he'll stay for quite some while." It was strange but she had got so used to Scrumpy now - he was just like she remembered her brother used to be - that she wasn't sure about seeing her real brother again. Suppose he was quite different.

That mysterious aunt called Aunt Penelope arrived one day bringing Harold with her. This aunt was tall, she wore a smart flowery dress and a large purple hat with feathers waving about on it, she laughed a lot with a strange deep laugh. Mollie felt decidedly wary of her. Harold seemed strange too at first because he seemed so different now, not at all what she had expected. She tried to ignore her strange new aunt - perhaps all aunts made you feel uncomfortable.

"Hello, funny face," Harold said, and she remembered he once used to call her that. They ran off laughing, chasing each other through the house and into the yard, round and round, over and under the beds, dodging behind chairs, hiding under a table, laughing and shouting. After that they got used to each other again.

"Are you staying here at home for ever now?" Mollie asked a few days later.

"No, I'm going home with Aunt soon." He insisted he wanted to go back home with Aunt Penelope to Blackpool, and not ever come back to live all the time in London.

"But home is here," Mollie protested.

"Why don't you come home with me?" he suggested. "I can have whatever I want, Aunt Penelope says so. She buys me lots of toys and new clothes. I'm going to be her boy in Blackpool and go to a proper school for boys."

"What's Blackpool like?" she asked. She thought it must be a place with a great big pond, very dark and mysterious.

"You won't fall in the pond, will you?" she asked. All she got for her concern for him was a shout of laughter, and a long explanation about the sea, and waves that ran after you and sand you could dig in to make castles. He painted a picture for her on a piece of paper but it just looked all yellow and blue stripes.

"They have electric trams to ride in and lots of lights."

"We have got lights and trams too."

"And there is a tower where they keep fish and wild animals."

"Grr," he growled as he chased her round the room again, pretending to be a lion or monkey, even an elephant.

"You'd never guess how big an elephant really is," Harold said. After that they often played wild animals together.

Then one day he went away again with Aunt Penelope. Mollie felt deserted. But she still had Scrumpy to play with, so she went upstairs and talked to him for a bit, and pretended to be a lion.

Chapter 6
Strange Experiences

Mollie gradually became aware of loud voices in the background, but it was sometime before she could drag her mind away from the past and back into the present. Strangers Corner, that was where she was. Hearing the sound of unfamiliar voices she set off to investigate, following the sounds to the back of the house. There she discovered various workmen wandering about measuring things.

"What are you doing here?" she demanded suspiciously, "I never gave anyone permission to come looking round this house."

"Your daughter asked us to come and measure things up for a new bathroom in case you might need one."

There they go again, doing things behind my back, Mollie thought angrily. Why had Mary taken upon herself to invite all these interfering builders to come poking round the house looking at things, interfering in her life? Why should anyone want to change the sleeping arrangements in that very high-handed way? Hadn't she herself made it plain enough that she would continue to sleep upstairs no matter who objected, so whatever were all these builders doing here?

"This is my house," she said to one of the men, "and I have given no one permission to come here. Will you please all leave at once."

The men went.

"Did you know about this Ned?" she asked aggressively as she saw him coming towards her.

"Nothing to do with me," he said defensively.

"You said," objected Mary, as she too appeared, "you remember you said we might ask what could be done with that back kitchen, in case you ever needed to sleep downstairs some day. In any case there are other things in the house that need looking at, damp patches, uneven floor tiles and so on."

"Dear me, and why should I ever want to change the back kitchen?" Mollie said angrily, "I said nothing of the kind."

"But I asked you," grumbled Mary, "and they only came to have a look."

"Well, I soon sent them packing, I told them they had no right to be on my property, snooping round the house like that. They won't be coming back in a hurry, I can tell you." She hoped Mary would be going home soon and then they could be left in peace.

"I'm going to make a cake," she announced.

All the family knew that when Mollie was really annoyed, she made a cake. In the past, when she still had the full use of her hands, she used to go off and play the piano for hours on end when she felt upset. But since her hands could no longer be persuaded to play, she made her famous fruit cake instead. After all it was one of the things she felt she could still do better than anyone else. Ned appreciated a cake - a light fruit cake for which she had a special recipe. She found cooking very difficult these days, what with her crooked hands, and her poor eyesight, but she could still manage a cake. Mary found her in the kitchen later, cigarette in the corner of her mouth as usual, and was ordered out again as soon as she offered to help.

"We'll be leaving in a few minutes," Mary said.

"Well, it can wait until after I've put this in the oven, can't it?"

While they waited for Mollie to finish the cake, Ned said rather sheepishly to Mary that she should go upstairs and find the necklace - a kind of family heirloom - that she had been told would be hers, and take it with her.

"Your grandmother always wanted you to have it, we all know that," he said, "and you never know, it might get lost or given away to someone else - anything might happen to it. It's yours, you know."

"I can't do that," said Mary, "she might miss it - it would feel like stealing."

Mollie reappeared having finished the cake and was very pleased to see the back of Mary and her family. She forgot about the cake, it was a bit burnt but most of it was edible. Ned could have a large piece at teatime. After all the hustle and bustle, things would go back to being ordinary again now. However, it did seem very quiet, almost eerie. Mollie was glad to go and feed the hens, they all came running as usual, and after the party there were plenty of scraps left over to feed them. She collected three eggs, that would do nicely for supper. She walked carefully back to the house, these days you had to be careful, it was so easy to knock against something, those old roots from the big oak tree, a can carelessly left when the hens' water tins had last been filled. You would think they would know better than to leave things about like that. There was something soothing in the cackle of the hens, and she lingered for a while, searching for more eggs laid in unlikely places. She really must get someone to cut down the nettles down there at the bottom of the run, they were getting out of hand.

When she got back to the house Ned was organising some papers, something to do with his meeting she supposed. The phone rang. Perhaps it was the call they had been waiting for, the news that was so long coming after all these years. But it was John who wanted to know how his father was.

"I was a bit worried about him yesterday," his voice said, "I wish I could have stayed another day to make sure he is all right. I think the heat was a bit much for him."

"He's a bit tired, a bit sleepy," she grumbled, "but that's nothing new. He never seems able to make much effort these days, it's not good for him to sit about so much."

"Has he seen a doctor yet?" the disembodied voice continued. "There are tests that need to be done. You promised you would make sure he went to see his doctor."

There they go again, thought Mollie. If it's not one of the children it's another, telling me I said this or that, making out I agreed to things I never knew about.

"Nonsense," said Mollie, "he just needs to make a bit more effort, that's all."

"Promise me to make sure he sees someone," John said. She could hear the worry in his voice.

"Oh, very well," she said. But she was tired, and she told herself there was nothing wrong with Ned, nothing that a few quiet days wouldn't put right. They are always trying to make out we are ill, when all we really need is sleep and quiet. What could they do anyway? I shan't let them take him off to hospital, that's for sure, that might be the end of him. Hospital treatment only made people worse she always found. He would have to go to that meeting, but she would see he had a proper rest after that.

Ned went out, and Mollie was alone again. Ned was good at meetings, everyone liked him, he knew how to organise things, meetings suited him. She hated official meetings herself, like the Women's Institute AGM she was supposed to attend. She had been a member for years, but refused to hold any official position in it. People at meetings were so pompous, so pleased with themselves. At meetings she would feel a sudden urge to disrupt things, shout fire, or start dancing, anything to lighten everyone's solemn mood.

It had always been like that. She remembered how irritating she had found her parents when she was young, their insistence on correctness. To be ordinary, she had discovered then, was also to be dull.

★

"You can't live in a world of your own making," her mother said to her once, after one of her escapades, when she pretended to run away from home. "Whatever you do has consequences, for you of course, but for the rest of the family too. Never forget that." But Mollie never could take people seriously. Relations, neighbours, the teachers at school, they all seemed at times to be like characters in a Dickens novel, so exaggerated, so much larger than life.

There was one of her uncles, Baba's brother, who sat at the piano playing loud music in his exaggerated way, throwing his head back exclaiming "roars of laughter, roars of laughter," after one of his musical jokes which neither she nor anyone else seemed to understand. She felt at home with him.

Going to stay with Aunt Penelope and Harold in Blackpool was supposed to be a holiday. The first time she went it was quite exciting, there were so many new things to see. Harold had been very pleased to show her his 'domain' - his toys, the seashore and the retreating waves, the animals in the tower, the pier, electric trams, firework displays, picture postcards, bright lights, bands playing, fair ground rides - all the excitement of something new and strange.

Besides, she and Harold were intrigued by the misuse of language. They still had that in common.

"So sorry, Mrs Winder, little Dorothy seems to have left the room on the carpet," set them giggling together after the departure of some embarrassed visitors.

They laughed together over Mollie's reporting of an overheard conversation in a dressmaker's shop,

"My dear if you insist on wearing that style you know perfectly well your lungs will drop out, a great mistake at your age, don't you think?"

Holidays in Blackpool never seemed quite ordinary. For one thing, it was difficult to know exactly what Aunt Penelope expected of her. She would ask Mollie to do one thing, then change her mind, and abruptly decide on something else. She often complained of headaches. She was full of sudden ideas which never seemed to work out the way they were supposed to do. She often asked Mollie to read to her, but in the middle of a chapter she would change her mind and Mollie would be asked to play the piano instead, or even find herself being hurried out on a sudden shopping expedition. Life could hardly be called predictable with Aunt Penelope. And Mollie was a little afraid of her uncle, who seemed cold and distant, but then he was a busy doctor and doctors, she supposed, had little time except for their patients. He was always explaining to Aunt Penelope that she must entertain his friends, wear fashionable clothes, keep the servants in order, help him to increase the number of his patients. Sometimes Mollie felt a bit sorry for her aunt.

When Mollie came back to London to stay with her parents, Harold sometimes came to stay with her, but he was restless, bored she supposed. His visits became shorter and less frequent. He grew more remote, became more and more of a stranger. But she still liked his jokes, even if he did treat her in that superior manner of his. It was always 'we do this in Blackpool', 'we do things this way' or 'we do it that way' - as if he was beginning to pity everyone living anywhere else, as if he thought of himself as a superior being living in a superior place. He's getting just like Uncle, she thought, distant and superior.

Soon it was as if she had two homes, one in Blackpool, and one in London. In London she spent a lot of time with her cousin Christine, who went to the same school. They had real fun together, acting out parts and dressing up in any discarded clothes they could find or borrow from their parents. Characters from books, imitations of their various relations, school teachers, witches, fairies, Kings and Queens, they tried them all. They made up little plays together. At family parties they played charades.

But just when she seemed settled again at school, she would be sent on the train back to Blackpool.

"You'll see" Banna would say, "you'll see it is important to get on with your uncle and aunt. They are well off, not like us, they have always promised to see you are well provided for. Your uncle owes me that much. All the money available when we were children was spent on his education rather than mine. He is the one who has a career to depend upon, he is the one who can provide you with an education and a marriage settlement."

More and more she was expected to read to her aunt and play the piano for visitors, she was taken out to supper parties, paraded like a daughter in front of their guests. She went to school sometimes for a week or two. Then she would be whisked away to help her aunt with some new plan or other. She was always glad to get home again to London.

Mollie often wished she could be an ordinary school girl like everyone else. It wasn't just that she missed so much school, or that she found her aunt so erratic, or that she found it increasingly difficult to decide whether she belonged in London or Blackpool. It was also that such strange things seemed to happen to her, things that happened to her and as far as she knew to nobody else.

For instance no one else she knew had ever seen a fairy. Once she had dared to tell Christine about fairy Marigold, but Christine thought she was making it all up. Mollie tried to make sense of it. After all, she told herself, there are very high and very low sounds that only animals and a few special people are able to hear, so why can't there be high and low things to see - things that some people can see and others can't. But she soon gave up the struggle to explain such things, even to herself.

Fairies, beautiful little fluttering creatures, came one night when she was alone in her room in Blackpool, gazing out of the window towards the shore. 'Once in a blue moon' meant a way of saying something would never ever happen, she always thought. But this night she really could see a blue moon. She had been restless and got out of bed to stand by the open window, watching the clouds float by in the ghostly light. She gazed at the white blossom of a tree which stood there in the garden. It, too, was now clothed in ethereal blue. The moon was blue, and the moonlight, an eerie beautiful blue light. It was strange how clear everything looked out there in that gentle blue haze. And dancing in that soft blue glow, there on the grass amongst the silvery blue cobwebs she could just make them out - those beautiful fairy creatures, almost transparent, almost but not quite impossible to see. They came flying and twisting in a dance through the branches of the tree, a dance so intricate it was difficult to know exactly where anyone of them was at any given moment.

She went down into the garden. There was no one about and she stood watching in fascination. It was like watching a little cloud of blue and silver, like an eerie flight of tiny birds, swirling around in the silvery blue. She put out her hand to see if she could touch them. One minute they were there, then next they had gone. For a brief moment she thought she could see them again, as if they were almost but not quite beyond her eyesight, just on the verge of disappearing again. They were remote, belonging to another world, but a world she wished she could join. How sad she felt when a few minutes later a cloud came over the moon, and the blue light disappeared. She went reluctantly back to bed. She never told anyone.

One day at home in London she talked to a primrose, or rather the primrose talked to her. She was lying flat down on her stomach, admiring the flower's delicate colour, looking to see if the flowers were either thrum-eyed or pin-eyed. They had been talking about them in a nature lesson in school the day before. She stared hard into the flower's centre which was, she saw, thrum-eyed. She could see the little orange tufts at the petal roots. She watched the shadows on the petals, admiring the soft yellow texture.

Then the flower suddenly grew bigger and bigger, she felt part of it, moving down the little funnel right into its very centre. I am a flower, she thought, I am a primrose. All round her was pale yellow and green, like a soft mattress she could sink into. I am a primrose, she thought, I have turned into a primrose. It was nice being a primrose.

When she heard a voice calling her, a far off hardly noticed sound which belonged to another world, she tried to ignore it. But it echoed through her brain, grew louder and more insistent, made her take notice of it, and she found herself no longer a primrose, but her ordinary self lying there on the ground.

"You'll catch your death of cold lying there on that damp grass," her mother scolded. Mollie wished she could have stayed being a primrose, everything was so clear, so beautiful, so timeless, another world. Now she knew what people meant when they said time could stand still. She didn't tell anyone.

After that she tried many times to make herself into a primrose again, and sometimes she almost succeeded, but it was never like the first time. She tried to be other flowers, she once tried to be a tree, but it never worked so well. You could only be a flower if you were not trying to be one, it just had to happen, she supposed. Being a flower was another of the secrets no one would ever believe.

She and her cousin Christine had great times together, dressing up in their mother's old clothes, trying on big hats and long gloves, pretending to be grown-ups, paying calls on neighbours, pretending to be other people. Christine would have a fit of the giggles sometimes, as they practised impersonating anyone they happened to meet that day. But Mollie always took the leading part. She knew she could almost become the other person, feel like them, talk like them, be them. Acting meant being in a kind of trance, she could forget about everything except being that someone else.

"A born actress," she overheard one of Banna's friends say after a Christmas game of charades.

"Guess who I am?" she would ask. And Christine and her cousin Steve, if he happened to be there, would be able to guess straightaway, often without a single word being spoken.

"Uncanny," Christine insisted. Mollie, especially was good at imitating all their various teachers. She would give Christine little tips on how to behave.

"Now then Christine," she might say in imitation of a particular teacher's voice, "you must learn to behave like a lady." School always seemed to be concerned with everyone being told to behave like ladies.

Mollie had been out shopping with Banna one day, riding on a horse bus to one of the big stores to buy some new school clothes. On the way home Mollie noticed a book left on one of the seats. It had a picture of a fairy on it.

"I found it, it was just lying there asking to be picked up," she told Christine defensively, as they walked home from school next day. "It didn't seem to belong to anyone, someone must have meant me to find it, how else could it have got on that seat in the bus. So I hid it under my coat. It can't have belonged to any ordinary person. Anyway I'm going to keep it."

The book said first of all that whoever found the book was never to tell anyone else about it, or something unpleasant would happen to them. Mollie decided it wouldn't matter if she told Christine, she was different. It had rhymes to summon fairies, and best of all lucky country charms, like how to cure warts, or make some man fall in love with you. They made various love potions from any of the plants they could find. Putting them in some of the teachers' drinks didn't seem to work very well but they went on trying. They used a charm to cure one of the girls of her warts and that was a success. They felt rather awestruck, perhaps spells did work after all. To cure warts you were supposed to spit in the place where ashes had been swept from the hearth and say some magic words. Soon they had a number of girls queueing up to have the same treatment, and much to their gratification it worked most of the time.

At home Christine often got into trouble for losing things, and for having such an untidy room. The book told them about poltergeists, and Mollie decided it must be a poltergeist, one of those naughty goblins - a mischievous sprite - who had got into Christine's room. It might move things about, the book said, or be busy hiding things, or throwing them round the room. What puzzled Christine most was when she knew she had put something somewhere, she was sure she had, but was unable to find it and yet the next time she looked there it was just where she thought she had left it in the first place. She knew she had looked for it there several times already. On the other hand she always seemed to find things quite easily when she used the lucky charm book for controlling poltergeists. Christine agreed about the poltergeist. Mollie said she had one in her room too.

"Mine throws things all over the room sometimes, and breaks things and no one believes me when I say it wasn't my fault."

One day they stood and gazed in horror as Mollie's bedroom began to shake, and things went flying everywhere - books fell off the shelves, paper flew round the table, bed clothes slithered to the floor, the soap dish fell off the washstand, while the jug standing in the basin wobbled and danced as if it were demented. Mollie and Christine stared at each other in horror. What they had only been half convinced of before, now became a certainty, there must be such things as poltergeists.

"Don't tell my father, will you?" said Christine in an awe-struck voice. Her father was a banker, much interested in local Protestant church affairs, he was also a lay preacher. He would have been angry at the very idea of believing in such things. Indulging in magic of any kind was to invite damnation. Christine in any case was never quite sure whether Mollie might not be playing tricks on her. Perhaps, she thought to comfort herself, Mollie was just playing a joke, though she couldn't see how she could have done that particular trick.

By this time Mollie had two younger brothers to play with, Francis, who scoffed at the very idea of magic, and little Arthur of whom she was especially fond. She spent hours trying to teach him to play the piano. He was too small to understand about magic. Boys never seemed to understand magical things in any case.

And then of course, there was that day she went to church with Christine and her parents, another strange day she would always remember. She had never been able to explain it, it was not the kind of thing you could talk about. She never mentioned it even to Christine. She would think she was making it up, or tell her there was something wrong with her brain. She was beginning to think Christine, who was already a bit wary of such strange experiences, might be right.

Christine always went to church with her parents on Sundays, and sometimes other days too. Christine's parents were very strict about religion, whereas her own parents only went to church occasionally, to marriages and christenings. That day she remembered was most perturbing. There she was kneeling in her pew, thinking about praying, and letting her mind wander, when everything round her disappeared, as if she were quite alone, removed to somewhere else. Only the somewhere else was still here, or nowhere, anywhere. She was so aware of herself that her surroundings seemed to have disappeared completely. Like being suspended on a star, bright and far away from everything, was the only way she could explain it to herself afterwards. Time seemed irrelevant, there was nothing but just being. She felt she was part of the great wide universe, but the universe was also her. She could have been there for seconds, hours, days, for all she knew. Time didn't seem to exist anymore.

She was being nudged by Christine, who said in a loud whisper it was time to sing a hymn. Mollie felt strange, as if she had come back from some very long journey and didn't quite recognise at first where she was.

"I've been floating about in the universe," she said, "whatever that is." Christine laughed, it was just like Mollie to be up to her tricks again. But Mollie never felt really quite ordinary after that. It was one of the things she wished would happen again, but it never did.

When Mollie was twelve, everything changed. She and Christine decided one day to dress up and go and call on the various local schools, including their own, pretending they were parents who had children they wished to enrol as pupils. They had a great afternoon. They were invited in to discuss details, given cups of tea, treated like real parents. They would emerge from each school laughing and giggling as they turned the nearest corner. But something must have gone wrong somewhere, because they were found out. Banna and she were summoned to her school next day. The headmistress was looking very stern as they were ushered into her room.

"I'm very sorry," the headmistress said, "but I have to tell you that Mollie does not seem to be the kind of girl we wish any longer to have at this school. We have spoken to Christine and her parents and from what we have heard it's not just the pranks that the two girls have been up to lately, dressing up and pretending to be parents. That in itself might be reprehensible, but she has also persuaded her cousin and other pupils to dabble in the idea of magic spells. A very unhealthy idea, particularly for girls at this impressionable age, I'm sure you will agree. Christine's parents are rightly horrified as would many other parents be should they get to know about what has been going on. We think it best that Mollie should leave the school straightaway." Mollie's feelings of guilt overcame her. She could see from her mother's face how upset she was. Even her father, usually the mildest of men, was angry when he heard about it. She never remembered her father being so angry ever before.

"We were only having a game," Mollie protested, "we weren't doing anyone any harm. You would think they could all take a joke. But the consequence was," she quoted to herself, as if from a line from a game of consequences, "that Mollie had to go and stay in Blackpool for ever." She was almost immediately packed off to go to school there, to be at the beck and call of her unpredictable aunt.

"After all, you'll be glad to be with Harold, won't you?" Banna said consolingly. Mollie was not so sure.

Chapter 7
No Tennis

The next day at Strangers Corner it was much cooler. Mollie felt more as if she belonged to the present.

"Thank goodness for fresh air," she muttered to herself. Up in the bedroom, as she looked out over the garden, the curtains were fluttering in the morning breeze. Ned was snoring as usual, it seemed more difficult than ever to rouse him. Perhaps she should persuade him to go and see a doctor after all.

But he woke with a start and insisted on going downstairs to fetch breakfast. He seemed all right. The smell of burnt toast was somehow comforting.

Things were much as usual, she had been imagining things, getting worried about nothing. They were still tired, both of them after the party and Ned's meeting and it always took a day or two to get back to their quiet uneventful way of life. They both just needed quiet and a rest, that was all.

"How was the meeting last night?" Mollie asked, as he appeared with the breakfast tray. He hadn't seemed to want to talk about it last night.

"Oh, all right," he answered. "They gave me this." It was a very handsome notebook, with his name embossed on the cover. "But I don't suppose I'll ever use it now."

Ned brought some letters with the breakfast, and they both looked eagerly for an unusual stamp or postmark. Most were bills, which Ned quietly spirited away - no need for Mollie to know how much they owed, how difficult things were just now. They would have to think about saying goodbye to the gardener, something would have to be done if they were to get through the next year. He would go over to Ruth's house later on and see what she might suggest. Perhaps she could take over the garden herself. Peter, her husband, could afford a gardener he supposed. After all they had been able to buy that land from him, the field that ran along the bottom of the garden. They might be glad of the extra produce a gardener could supply. That was all he could think of. He had already sold most of his assets - the surplus land - some pictures - some china. Mollie didn't seem to have missed anything, at least she didn't say so.

There was a letter from the Mason's hospital, asking him if he was sure he didn't want to go and have that prostate operation in the Masonic hospital. This he hastily and warily secreted, he was quite glad at times that Mollie couldn't see so well. He had told people at the hospital so many times now that he wasn't interested. It was different when he had first been for the check up - that was before Mollie had that stroke. Since then he knew he couldn't leave her, he must stay and look after her as long as he could. Besides he had left it so long he guessed it was too late now in any case. He hated the idea of operations and anaesthetics, he might be overheard saying things he wanted no one to hear. He hated the idea of losing control.

The hoped-for letter wasn't there, one which might lead to information about Mollie's long forgotten past. There was a Mr Henderson, a fellow Mason, whom he and Mollie once met when they briefly lived in London, whom Mollie now insisted might be able to provide some information. It seemed important for Mollie's sake to try and find the adopted boy if they could, to make some connection with her past. It was only in the last few months she had asked him what he could do to help, that she seemed to have been overtaken by a sudden and overwhelming desire to come to terms with the traumatic experiences of that runaway stay of hers in Belgium. She should have asked if he could be traced years and years ago, not left it until now when so many records would have been lost, and so many people would have died. She shouldn't have left it for so long he grumbled to himself.

"Don't worry, we'll hear soon. They told me they thought Mr Henderson's friends had been traced at long last, and they only have to make arrangements now for some further enquiries," Ned said. He hoped he was right, after all his friends in the Lodge had promised to do their best.

As the day wore on, the temperature rose again, and Ned became more sleepy. Mollie roused him now and again to reassure herself. He had said something about going over to see Ruth, but he said he would go and talk to her tomorrow - tomorrow would do. Well, it was hot, and tomorrow would do just as well. It was the weather, he would be his usual self again tomorrow. The day seemed very long. He felt very thirsty. Mollie kept making him cups of tea.

Eventually it got dark, and time to go to bed. Ned was already asleep breathing heavily, it took a long time before he would respond to her urgent nudges to get out of his chair. She had to admit that tonight she was really worried, for it soon became obvious that no way could Ned get up those narrow stairs to their bedroom. He tried, but each time he got his foot onto the first step, he couldn't pull himself up to the next one. She pushed, exhorted, told him to try sitting on each step in turn, but it was to no avail. She knew now she would have to call the doctor in the morning. His breathing was very heavy. He seemed to be so difficult to rouse.

All she could think of doing for tonight was to make up the bed for him in the tiny bedroom next door to the kitchen. It seemed very stuffy, so she aired it well, and somehow got him into the narrow single bed. He seemed wandering a bit, talked as though he had too much to drink, although she knew he hadn't. She was worried, for the first time since he was wounded in the First World War, she was really worried about him. There had been times - like the time he went swimming in one of those clay pits and couldn't get out, or the time he insisted on riding with the children and had fallen off and lain in bed moaning and groaning for the next few days - there had been times like that when she felt concerned. But this was something more serious, now he might be really ill.

Then she decided she couldn't leave him downstairs on his own all night, he might need her. He might need a drink, anything. There was no room in that narrow bed for two, no room even for another mattress on the floor next to the bed. She brought bedclothes down and lay outside his door on the cold hard boards, listening even while she dozed to Ned's heavy breathing. At least he was sleeping. She would call the doctor first thing in the morning.

With the morning came Ruth, tut-tutting at the situation, arranging for Ned to go into hospital, for Mollie to go to bed with warm drinks and a sedative. Ruth uttered not a word of criticism, Mollie would rather she had. Then she found herself alone in the house again, dozing in bed, not knowing what was happening at the hospital, waiting for news, not knowing where everyone had gone. She hated being alone.

When she was sufficiently awake again, and with some difficulty, she rang the hospital. It was thoughtful of Ruth to have left the number by the phone. All the information she was given when at last she got through to the ward was that Ned was comfortable, whatever that might mean. Just like a hospital to tell you nothing at all. They said she could visit him in the afternoon. The hours went by slowly as she dozed on and off, her clouded mind meandering through past history again.

★

She had been sent back to Blackpool when she was twelve, her brother Harold was by then fourteen. The next three years she thought of as the lost years of her childhood, those dreary years with her uncle and aunt, and her increasingly aloof brother. She felt that she didn't belong anywhere. Nobody really seemed to want her. She lived in a kind of no man's land. There she was, banished from home, compelled to live with her indifferent uncle, and her unpredictable aunt. They had by then formally adopted Harold as their own son, but she was just still only their niece. To begin with she and Harold would do things together - go for long walks along the sands for example, but that soon changed. He never seemed to be at home anymore, but was off with what she had labelled his rackety school friends. She didn't really blame him for that. She tried to get on with him, thought up jokes to tell him, suggested things they could do together. As they grew older she tried mentioning subjects she thought might seem important to him, he liked to think of himself as grown up and superior - politics - religion - the kind of things she sometimes managed to read about in the papers. But he was not in the least interested in her or what she had to say, only annoyed when her uncle occasionally gave him a lecture about not looking after her as a brother should. She supposed her brother was no different from anyone else.

She must have tried once too often to find something they could both talk about, he was nearly seventeen by then she remembered. Impatiently he said she wouldn't understand the kind of things that mattered to him now. He rattled off such a long list of bewildering ideas that she was left completely nonplussed.

"It's exciting," he said, "isn't it, to think of petrol automobiles being driven round the countryside? Soon there won't be anymore need for horses."

How could a girl realise the advantage of shaving with the new safety kind of razor, instead of the cut-throat variety? Did she know anything about the causes of the South African war? Had she heard that Marconi had invented a wireless, a way of talking to other people across long distances by using waves in the air? Did she know what radioactivity was, and X-rays? Did she think workers in England should have old age pensions like they now did in Germany? Did she know what a motion picture was? Mollie felt truly put in her place. Waves in the air, invisible rays, moving pictures, he must be making it all up. After that she gave up her attempts to talk to him about anything that seemed to matter.

She was supposed to attend school but was never there because she was kept at home to do her aunt's bidding. Notes would be sent saying Mollie was wanted at home, or she wasn't well, or was away. Any excuse seemed to be accepted by the school.

"I don't know why we bother to pay the fees," her aunt said one day.

"I'm under an obligation to my sister to see that she is sent to a good school and we must see that she is," her uncle said firmly. So she was sent back to school for a week or two, even started to make a few friends. But first once a week, then twice, then almost always she had to stay at home with Aunt for one reason or another. Especially to read to her.

There was pleasure in reading, in inventing the voices of the imagined characters in the books. She learnt to change her voice to match each one, it was like acting, pretending to be all kinds of different people. That and playing the piano for her own pleasure, made life more tolerable.

"You really are quite good at the piano Mollie, I'm sure you could be up to the standard of any concert pianist. We must get some advanced lessons for you," Aunt said one day. "I know someone we could ask." But of course nothing was ever arranged. Mollie did decide there and then however she would like to be a concert pianist, and spent still longer hours playing music to herself.

She seldom went out during the day except to accompany her aunt on shopping expeditions. She liked speeding along the front on the electric tram - there was the sight of the giant wheel against the skyline as it carried its passengers aloft - the busy crowds round the entrance to the piers and along the promenade - the occasional sound of music from the dance halls, but these could only be enjoyed from a distance, she was never part of them. At night there would be bright lights, fireworks, more sounds of music as she was whisked past them all on her way to one of the houses where a dinner was being given by a friend or an uncle. Once or twice she was taken to the theatre, she only wished it could have been more often. She seldom saw anyone her own age. Soon she ceased to see anyone from school. She often felt she was only tolerated as a kind of servant to her aunt, to carry her shawl perhaps, read to her, open the door for her as she strode restlessly through the house.

The people at the dinner parties all seemed so old, and they talked above her head of things she knew little about. In fact she was beginning to think she knew very little about anything. She felt so embarrassed by her ignorance that once or twice she tried to read the newspapers which her uncle had delivered every morning. She was always careful to make sure she left them exactly as she found them, otherwise she knew she would get into terrible trouble. She knew he could not bear anyone to touch his paper until he had finished with it, which might take days. She once or twice tried to join in the dinner party conversation with what little information she had gleaned, but she was quickly put in her place. Fred the butler would keep discarded copies of the papers for her to read, but the information was always out of date. Fred and Cook were the only people she could ever discuss things with.

Harold was busy with his own pursuits now he was older, girls mostly, Mollie guessed, more aloof than ever. After he left school and started working at a bank he seemed to have lots of arguments with Uncle and Aunt. He did find time occasionally however, in his condescending way, to make jokes which might make her laugh. That at least was something.

> I said to her Mabel
> You look well in sable
> But I like you best in your bear (bare) skin.

Now why should she suddenly remember his saying that? Perhaps because at the time she began to realise he was much more interested in various girls than in anything else. She longed to join in his activities, going to parties where there would be people of her own age. Perhaps he felt his friends were not the kind of people she ought to meet. He talked about a tennis club where he played sometimes. But he never suggested she should join him.

"But I used to play sometimes when I was at school in London, I can play quite well, really, why don't you let me try?"

"You'll have to ask Aunt about that," was all he would say. He obviously didn't want her to cramp his style.

Some of her happiest times had been those she spent in the kitchen. There was Fred the butler who taught her how to clean the silver with old newspapers, until everything shone with that special soft glowing light he took such pride in maintaining. Nancy the cook provided her with an approach to cooking she found invaluable in years to come. She learnt for instance how to make parkin, a cheap and filling cake made with oatmeal : '8 ozs oatmeal, 8 ozs flour, 8 ozs golden syrup, 2ozs sugar, lard, milk, ginger', she would chant to herself, years later, as she struggled to cook for her own large family. She could almost hear the tone of Cook's voice- 'You need only a ham bone, lentils, left over vegetables, and lots of dumplings to make a tasty stew.' 'Treacle tart will soon satisfy any boy's appetite; any kind of leftovers and a bit of potato can be made into tasty bubble and squeak; you can always make something out of nothing, you just need a little imagination.' They often experimented together. She helped with the washing and ironing. She felt at home, at least she was appreciated 'below stairs.'

Cook had a great reputation as a fortune-teller. She could, she said, read palms, or decipher the future in a tea cup. She was said to have made an astounding number of correct forecasts for her friends. Sometimes when Uncle and Aunt were out for the evening Cook and Fred would invite friends in. They would congregate in the kitchen round the warm kitchen range drinking cups of tea.

"We're in for one of them sessions," Fred would say. "Not that I believe in all them things." But he listened just the same.

One evening Cook told Mollie's fortune. Mollie didn't know what to make of it, and she certainly didn't want all of it to be true.

"You will travel," Cook said. "I can see a long journey for you very soon." Mollie liked that bit.

"You'll see much happiness and much sorrow in your long life," Cook continued. "And what is this I see? You'll spend many years of your life searching for something you have lost."

"Will I ever find it again?" Mollie asked, despite herself.

"Yes, but not for many many years. The leaves tell me it will be a long search."

Mollie didn't like the last bit. She agreed with Fred, she decided she didn't really want to believe in fortune telling.

It was to Fred and Cook, as she helped in the kitchen, that she expressed her frustrations - her longing to join the tennis club, to go to parties where everyone was not so old, to have some fun with real friends as she used to have in London with her cousin Christine. Christine and she had been forbidden to write to each other, and though she tried sending letters secretly, she never got a reply.

"I wish I could just be a schoolgirl," she said to Cook one day. " All I want is to go to school and have friends like everyone else. I just want to be ordinary."

She lived in two worlds, 'below stairs', where criticisms of 'society' were often expressed, even criticism of her aunt. But there was never a word said against her uncle, he was such a good doctor, so ready to help anyone. Upstairs, entertaining and being entertained were her aunt's occupations, following all the conventions of an aspiring polite society. Mollie, while despising what she considered her uncle and aunt's social pretensions, still found herself amused at the incongruous remarks of some of their more unsophisticated acquaintances.

"Prick all of them sausages over with a fork," their hostess shouted down to the cook once when they had been invited out by one of her uncle's newly rich friends. Cook and the butler would have been just as amused as she was at such uncouthness. Yet Mollie much preferred Mrs Spade, as she dubbed this lady, to many of their other acquaintances, with their mincing speech, exaggerated hats, spiteful gossip, or with their tales of society friends of which Mollie believed not a word.

"You have heard, I dare say, about the visit of Sir William to my dear cousin Oliver. Such a nice man, we had such an interesting conversation."

"The Bishop says he hopes to come to my little party next week, a Bishop no less, my dear. Of course I will have to be very careful about what other guests I invite."

"The Lord Lieutenant is likely to grace our charity ball next month. Quite a responsibility you know, but then I've had plenty of experience concerning the correct etiquette."

Mollie amused herself sometimes by inventing new names for them all, like Plumley or Hopeful, Twittering or Spiteful. It was one way of surviving those interminably boring dinners.

Then there was another world, a world of clandestine excursions. Mollie would finish whatever she had been told to read to her aunt - Dickens, or Scott perhaps, letting her voice trail off to nothing. Assured Aunt was really asleep, she would at first just go to her own room. But when she didn't get sent for again, or scolded for her absence, she started quietly letting herself out of the house. She would go down to the pier and watch the waves on the sea front. Music was usually being played by the band there. She was soon caught because Aunt woke up one day and wanted her for something before she had time to return. There was a row of course.

"I am responsible to your parents for seeing you come to no harm," she said. "I can't have you going off like that on your own." For once her uncle backed Mollie up in the ensuing recriminations. He was a good doctor, even if he was not really very interested in her.

"Mollie needs some exercise at her age, or she will start getting some ailment or other. An afternoon walk will do her good," he insisted.

"I don't like the idea of her roaming about along the sea front on her own," Aunt said, "no young lady should behave so. Besides there are some rather unsavoury characters about these days you know. All those factory workers who come here for their holidays, a rough lot I'm told. It isn't right for her to be out on her own."

"Then go with her, for goodness sake."

"You know how uncertain my health can be, I need my afternoon rest, you said so yourself."

"Then for heaven's sake arrange for someone else to go with her," her uncle said, exasperated. Mollie was delighted. Now she was allowed to go out walking with one of her aunt's younger friends, a lady called Mrs Dora Darling. They set off each afternoon while her aunt had her rest.

Mrs Darling was only too pleased to take advantage of the situation which thus presented itself so obligingly to her. She had wanted for sometime to find a way of meeting an admirer without danger of discovery. The arrangement suited them all very well. Mollie would go down to the pier or to the Tower concert room, where a band would be playing, while her 'chaperone' would meet with her 'friend.' They arranged to meet up and walk together as they returned, so as not to arouse suspicion about their separate activities.

Mollie did so like that concert band. She watched the band leader, romantic Tom. She smiled at the pleasant recollection she still had of him, despite everything. She remembered what a very handsome man she had thought him, as she saw him up there on the platform conducting the music - his quick movements - dark eyes and a little moustache - his gentle voice - she even imagined he looked a little like her brother in some ways.

There came the day when he asked for a volunteer from the audience to play the piano with the band, Mollie offered to try and got a lot of applause for her efforts. After that she was often persuaded to take part. Even Mrs. Darling applauded when she came back early one day and heard her playing.

She got to know the members of the band quite well. There were about twenty of them all together, although some came and went in a rather bewildering fashion. There was the violin player called Sid, small and wiry with an Irish accent; Ronnie, tall and lugubrious, who played the clarinet; and then there was Ted, the drummer, with his perpetual silly jokes and artificial laughter. Paul played the banjo and sang comic songs, though sometimes he would play the accordion.

Sadie was their usual piano player, and she occasionally sang comic songs as well. She often complained of feeling tired. Sadie was the one who patched up the frequent disputes among the players, saw that everyone had their music, complained on behalf of the players when the food at their lodgings was inedible. The cellist was called Donnie and the viola player was Connie, they were married, and had a little girl called Bonnie - what a comical collection of names Mollie thought - Donnie, Connie and Bonnie. Bonnie was sometimes brought on the stage. She was still too young to play the piano very well, but the audience would applaud heartily when she did. Sometimes she sang a song, she had rather a sweet babyish voice.

The band played marches, popular songs, waltzes for people to dance to, they varied the programme according to the audience. Mollie felt light-hearted when she was with the band; she loved to listen, but was especially pleased when she was asked to play with them.

Chapter 8
Escapade

"End of the season," Tom announced abruptly one day, after one of the performances. "We've only got two more weeks before we leave to go on our next continental tour. Of course it's just possible we may come back here for next year's season," he added. But she didn't quite believe him. She must have looked as devastated as she felt, and he put his arm round her, which made her tingle all over and feel soft inside. She felt very awkward, what an embarrassing, unexpected thing for him to do.

"We shall miss our little pianist," he said, "but every year when the season finishes here, we try our luck on the continent. This year we are going to Belgium - Bruges to start with. We enjoy our continental tours, don't we Sadie?" he asked. Sadie said of course they did but didn't look entirely enthusiastic. Mollie must have looked as unhappy as she felt, for now once again she was to lose some new-found friends.

"Perhaps you would like to come and help me sort out some of the music for the tour, there is a lot to do before we leave," Tom said. He led her round to the back of the stage, and there out of sight of everyone else, he kissed her full on the lips. Just like that... She felt so strange, so helpless, she had never felt like that before. She never knew people could have such strange agitated feelings. Besides it was as if all her frustration and unhappiness had just melted when he kissed her. Instead she was enveloped by a hollow excited feeling, a longing for that moment to linger on for ever. She was a willing participant, wanted more, needed to be wanted, to be thought worthy of his attention. She loved the excitement, her tingling senses, that sinking feeling. At the same time she felt somewhat bewildered, not sure what to make of it all.

"How old are you?" he asked surprisingly. What had age got to do with it, she thought?

"Seventeen," she lied. Well, fifteen was nearly seventeen, wasn't it? She wanted him to treat her as if she were grown-up. Sadie appeared with more music to sort out.

"Will we see you tomorrow Mollie?" Tom asked tentatively, as he turned away from her. Mollie just nodded as she walked away, trying to understand all these new strange sensations. When they got home that day she discovered she and Mrs. Darling had been discovered in their little deception. Someone had recognised Mollie playing the piano and had mentioned it to Aunt, who was of course furious.

"We make arrangements for you to go for walks in the afternoon and this is how you repay us, appearing in public with a concert band. How could you disgrace us so?"

Mrs Darling was accused of deceit and treachery, but protested that she thought there was no harm in it.

"You mean to say," criticised Aunt, "you just sat there in the audience watching Mollie make a fool of herself. How could you? I trusted you to look after her."

Dora Darling looked beseechingly at Mollie. Mollie had no intention of betraying her friend, the least said the better.

"I told you it was not a good idea," Aunt said to her uncle when they were discussing the situation together later, "I knew it would end in tears."

"Don't blame me," he answered, "you could at least have found her a more reliable companion."

It all seemed to Mollie rather like a scene out of one of the romantic novels she sometimes read to her aunt, secret assignations, jealous husbands, tears and recriminations.

The result of all the turmoil was that she was to be allowed to join the tennis club instead of going for walks.

"Better exercise for her anyway," Uncle said. As Mrs Darling was a member of the club and because she was such a friend of Aunt, and because she was rich and because she promised to ensure that Mollie in future always behaved in a ladylike fashion, she was forgiven her past indiscretion.

So Dora Darling was deputed to accompany Mollie when she went to play tennis at the club. Aunt took Mollie shopping to buy all the right clothes - Aunt was very particular about clothes - and they spent a long time finding a suitable tennis racket. Within a week all arrangements had been made. Such expectations Mollie now had of this new experience, she was looking forward to a wonderful afternoon.

Perhaps she wouldn't miss the band so much if she could play tennis and find some friends her own age. In any case, she wasn't yet sure how she really felt about Tom. His presence would now be so disturbing, perhaps it was just as well she would no longer be able to see him.

She had walked past those grass tennis courts many times, you could see what was going on through the hedge, she had watched them play, listening to the shouts and laughter that came floating over the bushes.

How pleased she was, the day she was to join the club, so full of pleasure at the thought. Before she set out dressed in her new tennis outfit, she twirled several times in front of the mirror admiring the effect. She looked well enough, she thought, for someone to want to play with her. If she felt a bit shy, at least she would have Dora with her.

"I'm glad you're coming with me," Mollie said, as they set out. "Aunt says you'll introduce me to everyone."

"Hmm," Dora said uncomfortably, "I hope you don"t mind my dear if I don't come with you straight away. This is an important day for me you see, I haven't seen my friend for the past few days and I need to see him urgently to explain, and I promised I'd be there early today. I'll come and join you later, we'll need to walk home together afterwards in any case. We can't risk being found out again, can we?" she said teasingly.

Mollie felt deserted of course, but what could she say? It was the one day she felt she really needed the company of her 'chaperone', but she didn't like to say so and she knew it was no good to protest anyway. They had promised to keep each other's secrets after all.

So there was nothing for it but to brave the club on her own. She found a bench to sit on by one of the courts, and sat there feeling eyes staring at her in curiosity, feeling more and more conspicuous. As the minutes ticked away, some new arrival would glance across at her, and her hopes would rise only to be dashed. A man and a woman walked by, obviously looking at her in curiosity, laughing together she imagined at her expense. Once a man walked towards her and she started to stand up to greet him, but then she saw he was making for someone else close by. But mostly she was just ignored. She sat there in misery until Dora eventually returned.

"Sorry I was so long," said Dora, "You know how it is. I suppose we must be getting back now. Had a good afternoon?" It was all Mollie could do not to burst into tears then and there.

When she got back she went straight up to her room where she could cry in peace. She would never ever go back to that club, she would never again risk being so humiliated. She took off her tennis things and threw them under the bed. She ignored her aunt's protests and cajoling from behind her locked door. She said she didn't feel well. She worked out a plan of revenge against the world. She told Aunt she had a headache. She kept her bedroom door locked.

Next day to all outward appearances was much like any other day. She had breakfast. She tidied her room. She played the piano, read a book. After lunch she put on her tennis clothes. She waited for Dora, and they set out together.

"Enjoy your tennis," Aunt said as they left

"I can come with you today," Dora said.

"You can go to the tennis club on your own then," Mollie retorted. "If you tell on me, I'll tell on you. I want to be on my own."

That fateful day, she was after all only fifteen, she went along to where she knew the band would be playing. She just had to see Tom.

"What's up?" he asked, "and why the tennis outfit?" Mollie felt tears in her eyes, despite herself. "You do look so unhappy, you poor little thing. Anything we can do?" he asked, putting his arm round her. She stood there thinking that at least somebody cared about her, realised how unhappy she was. Oh how comforting that arm was.

Had she quarrelled with anyone? Was she ill? Where was her family? Had she been turned out of her house? he asked, the questions tumbling out one after the other. She shook her head at each new suggestion. He turned her round and looked straight into her eyes. It was at that moment, she thought in later years, that the events of the next part of her life were finally decided. There seemed no point just then in explaining anything to him. If she told him the whole story he would probably just take her back to her aunt. Besides, he might decide he didn't like her anymore when he discovered what a well-known doctor her uncle happened to be. Much better to make up a plausible story, so that there would be no need to explain anything at all.

Oh how happy she felt with his arm round her. She didn't care about not playing tennis with those stupid people at the tennis club. She needed Tom.

It was easy, Tom seemed to believe every word she said. She explained she was an orphan, lived in some lodgings, paid for by a very distant uncle whom she never saw, who resented having to pay for her keep. Her parents had been quite well off and she had been to a girls' school in the south of England before they died two years ago. But then there was no money left, and she was sent up here to earn her keep as a seamstress. She became quite eloquent describing how she hated the establishment she had been sent to. How she quarrelled with the supervisor, and how she decided never to go there again.

"I have no idea what will become of me," she said in her best pathetic romantic novel style. The story was near enough the truth, she could not be more unhappy than the girl she had invented. Tom obviously believed every word of it.

Tom was quiet for quite a while.

"How would you like to join the band?" he asked suddenly. He must have seen how pleased she was. He immediately started talking about making plans.

"We could do with another pianist, Sadie is finding she can't do as much as she used to. You could teach Bonnie the piano too. I dare say we could support another player. Sadie will look after you, show you the ropes. We have all got used to your being with us over the last few months, you seem to fit in so well with everyone. We could do with some fresh inspiration too. What do you say?" He spoke in a breathless kind of way, as if he had just decided something and needed to say what he was going to say in a great hurry before he changed his mind. There was a long pause. She would be found out if she played for the band again.

"We leave in a few days time for our continental tour, I told you that, didn't I? We're catching the night boat train for Dover next Thursday. Why don't you come with us? From what you say you have nothing to lose. I'll look after you, we all will." Mollie hesitated at such a grand idea, but it didn't take long for her to make up her mind. What had she got to lose? Besides she was so very fond of Tom. She knew then that whatever he asked, even if it meant going to far away, unknown places like Africa or China, she would gladly have said yes. She felt even more like a heroine out of one of those romantic novels she read to her aunt.

So everything was arranged - she would join Tom and the rest of the band at the station on Thursday evening, when they were all to embark on the night train for the crossing to Ostend. She didn't really know where Ostend might be, except it was across the English Channel somewhere in Belgium. It sounded so exciting to be travelling abroad. She was to bring her luggage and Tom would have her ticket ready for her. There was no need for any other papers, he said, she would travel with the band. She remembered Cook had predicted she was going to travel abroad. It suddenly seemed quite the natural thing to be doing.

She worked out for herself what she considered a very daring plan, it was like the stories she had read of people running away to Gretna Green to get married. Uncle and Aunt were to be out that evening, she already knew that, and they usually didn't come home until the early hours. She would have her supper, play the piano for a while as she often did. It would be foolish to arouse any suspicion.She would say she was going to bed quite early - that would mean she would have plenty of time to pack the two suitcases that had luckily been kept stored in her room ever since she had come here. She would take the sheets from her bed and knot them together, then tie on the suitcases and lower them quietly out of the window. Then she would climb down herself. Fred and Cook would be likely to have an early night - they often did when her uncle and aunt were out late. No one would suspect a thing as long as she was really quiet. No one would miss her until next morning when she would be on her way to a foreign country. It was such a perfect plan. No one would have the slightest suspicion as to where she had gone, or with whom.

She couldn't think how anyone could possibly have any idea where she was going. Fancy being able to disappear, so that no one you knew would ever have the slightest idea of your whereabouts. She could become a new person, she would find herself a new name, no one would ever find her. Nor of course would anyone really miss her, not Aunt, not Uncle, not Harold, not her parents, not even Fred and Cook after a short while. She could start all over again, make lots of new friends, lead an exciting new kind of life. When the church clock struck nine, she would escape, free at last to do whatever she wanted to do.

She went over the plan again in her mind, she couldn't see how anything could go wrong. She did think of leaving a note but decided against it. She was someone else now, an escaping orphan, so what was the use of saying anything that might inadvertently give anyone a clue as to where she might be. She would be a new person. She would tell everyone in the band to call her Meg, from now on she would be Meg.

Thursday evening came, and it all worked out better than she could have imagined. True, the suitcases got stuck as she lowered them gently, dangling at the end of the knotted sheets, and for a few palpitating moments she thought someone would hear them bumping on the wall. But nothing happened, no sound of a door, no voices, just the quiet night. She scraped her knee as she scrambled down after the cases, but no matter. Now she was free. Her racing heart had made her breathless. She picked up the cases, wondering if, perhaps even half hoping, expecting, that someone would see her. But no, the street was empty, and then she was gone, leaving the sheets dangling out of the window at the back of the house.

At the station she was greeted with much friendliness by all the players. Sadie said she was delighted, said Mollie must sit next to her on the journey. There was all the usual noise and bustle, whistles and clanking trains, lights and dark shadows. She was shepherded aboard a green puffing giant of a train, and subsided into the corner seat of the carriage with a feeling of total unbelief.

That first night on board the boat was probably the happiest most carefree and exciting time she had ever experienced in her whole life. There on the deck, with Tom's arm round her, love was in the wind as it danced between them, love was in the stars and the brightness of eternity, love was in the soothing murmur of the waves, echoing back the mysteries of the sea. The lights of the land slowly retreated, a path of yellow moonlight beckoned them towards the farther shore. She would know the enchantment of love that night, the oneness of earth and sky locked in the oneness of two beings. That was how it seemed to her. The pleasure of it all - the romance, her exuberant feelings, what a magical night to remember, ethereal, that was the right word, it felt ethereal, like flying away with the fairies into fairyland. Even the moon was welcoming her to a new life. There never could be another night like this.

When Tom kissed her, sea and air and sky and stars and Tom all fused into one moment of happiness. She could refuse him nothing, even had she wanted to, how could she when her whole body ached for the same things as his. This was real life, this was what love was about, this abandonment to the pleasures of the night. And now she supposed they would be spending the rest of their lives together. Perhaps he would ask her to marry him. Love was a wonderful thing. Two people joined as one, two people sleeping in each other's welcoming arms.

Next day they were in a foreign country, she was with Tom and she was starting on her great adventure. There was so much to see and do, so many new experiences to revel in. Mollie enjoyed those months of travelling round the Belgian countryside, everything was new and exciting. Besides now Tom was there beside her, especially at night.

She enjoyed the company of the players, and was amused and entertained by their constant petty quarrels. She admired Sadie, who organised everything, and never seemed to get annoyed herself.

"Sadie, may I have a word with you? You know I'm entitled to a bigger room than Sid. I've been longer with the band so could you please tell him to change rooms with me."

"It's not my turn to sort the music this morning, I did it last time."

"Sadie, why don't you tell Ronnie he should smarten up a bit? I can't stand that long face of his any longer. He'll scare away the audience with that gloomy expression."

Mollie wondered sometimes if that was how wars had started, with frustration and stupid little quarrels over nothing at all. Such small matters produced far more heated arguments than problems which really mattered, like finding one night, because of a mix up, that no accommodation had been provided for them. They had spent the night amicably together in a barn. No doubt, she thought to herself, they grumble about me behind my back. But they were very kind to her. She enjoyed playing to a new kind of audience. It was a good time.

She thought at first she would be followed, that someone would be bound to find her, come to take her back to Blackpool. She used to imagine with some satisfaction the panic her departure might have caused. They would be frantic about her whereabouts, because as Uncle Arthur had said so often, he felt responsible for her to her parents. That will take the satisfied smile off his face, that will make everyone realise how unhappy they made me, she thought vindictively. He and Aunt Penelope had no idea how she felt. It was obvious her own parents didn't really care about her anymore. If they had, they would have come to take her home to London long ago, after she had written those unhappy letters to them. Harold wouldn't care, he would be quite pleased to have her out of the way. She felt more than ever lately that he just thought her an inconvenient nuisance.

But she soon found she wasn't really bothered how any of them might think, even Fred and Cook she knew would soon forget about her. They might have minded a bit when they discovered she was gone, but not for long. She imagined them there in the kitchen discussing her disappearance, hoping she was safe. But they would soon find something else to talk about. Fred and Cook faded from her mind, like everyone else.

Chapter 9
Romance

I'm becoming obsessed with the past, Mollie thought, her mind returning with an effort to the present. She supposed it was because there was nothing much else to think about now. Ned was in hospital. Running away had been so easy in those days. Nowadays if you wanted to travel there were regulations, and passports were needed. Going off to Belgium with Tom had been so simple, no one had even asked her to prove how old she was.

She could smell burning, she must have left the kettle on in the kitchen. When she went to look it was glowing red hot. She better not tell Ruth, she would be so cross about it. She turned off the gas. She would have to wait a long time before everything cooled down again. It wasn't the first time she had forgotten about a kettle.

Two of her grandchildren, Timmy and Phylidda clattered into the house.

"I suppose you know you have burnt a hole in the bottom of the kettle?" Timmy said accusingly. "You should never leave the gas on unless you are watching it, you know what Mum says. I'll tell her to get you a new one."

"We just came in to see how you are, we're just off to play tennis at the club," Phyllida said. She really did look rather smart dressed in white tennis clothes.

"Mum says she will be driving you to the hospital today, she'll be round about two o'clock. Give our love to Grandpa when you see him." They gave her a brief kiss, and they were gone.

Mollie looked out at the garden and to the field beyond. She wished she was playing tennis herself. It wasn't just that fiasco at the tennis club in Blackpool, all those years ago, although that was the start of it. She had meant to build a tennis court in her own garden, to learn to play the game properly. Except for the years during the First World War, she and Ned always had a house with a big enough garden. The field would have made a very good tennis court. But there had been other things to consider, children demanding attention, lack of money and the struggle to make ends meet. The tennis court had always seemed to come at the bottom of the list. As the years had gone by she still had visions of herself running round a court dressed in white, making graceful strokes as the ball bounced at her feet. Well some things are never to be. At present she would just like to be able to watch others playing out there. I suppose if I hadn't run away, it might have been different. All those might-have-beens. But she had run away with all the consequences that followed.

★

Those consequences had certainly been dramatic. Travelling abroad seemed so exciting at first, the boat, the trains, the people, the places, they all came crowding back into Mollie's memory. There was a lot of travelling. The band seldom stayed in one place more than a few weeks. Liege, Antwerp. Brussels, Ghent, Namur, she soon felt she knew the whole of Belgium. She didn't much care for those wide expanses of heavy soil, the coal mines and their spoil heaps which dotted the landscape - so flat and monotonous, anonymous, smelling all the time of mud and coal. Little rises, hardly high enough to be called hills, little ditches, sometimes little clumps of trees, then more flat fields. Now and again there would be a straight line of poplars standing sentinel over one of the low sprawling farm houses afloat on those endless fields. Yes, if anyone ever mentioned Belgium she knew exactly what that countryside looked like.

What a strange thing it was to see those little milk carts pulled along by dogs. The dogs didn't seem to mind. Mollie liked the dark clothes the women with their wide white starched head-dresses and white aprons; she liked watching the old women as they sat on their doorsteps, their pincushions in front of them, making those intricate lace patterns with their dancing bobbins.

She found the language a bit harsh to her ears, but she soon learned to speak it. It wasn't so different from the little French she had acquired at school. Walloon was the name of the native language and Tom insisted on calling it that 'Wallowing Patois.' She was much better at it than the rest of the band, and they soon made her their interpreter. She enjoyed talking to many of the country folk they met, it gave her a feeling of satisfaction to think she was becoming someone else, a new personality. It was part of her developing identity as Meg. She hoped she might one day be looked upon as a native Belgian rather than as a runaway English girl. Then no one would ever find her.

It was a bohemian kind of life. They lived mostly on stew and potatoes and bread, they stayed in many dingy rooms, sometimes got moved on when funds became too low. It was a type of existence which seemed at the time to suit Mollie very well. "It's the gypsy in you," Tom said.

'My mother said, I never should
Play with the gypsies in the wood.
If I did, she would say
Naughty girl to run away'

Mollie quoted, as they smiled at the rhyme together. She might not have much liked the smell of the fields, but she disliked the smell of the towns even more. She got used to it though. Insanitary her uncle would have said. After a time you don't notice something like that, it's so pervasive. She liked the town houses, tall and solid with tiers, usually three, of narrow symmetrical windows, and often those tiny little dormer windows high up in the grey short pitched roofs. She would imagine the people up there spying on the world far below, living their secret lives behind their little windows. A comfortable feeling such buildings give you she thought, solid lives lived behind solid walls.

She played in most of the performances when there was a piano available - otherwise Paul would play the accordion. When Mollie played she played with a flourish, imagining herself as a world famous pianist, inventing mannerisms and adding trills and frills to the music as Tom encouraged her to do. Sometimes the band played little tunes she made up for them. She gave Bonnie piano lessons. She began to think of herself as a musician.

Sadie insisted she wore what she called more relevant clothes that made her look older and more sophisticated. They slept in rundown rooms, in sleazy districts, although Tom and Sadie took great care to protect her from the unwanted attentions of other men. She belonged to Tom now. As the winter progressed it got colder and colder. Occasionally, when times were good, they lived in relative comfort. Sometimes there seemed hardly enough to eat, sometimes they went out for a celebration and drank champagne which made her feel even more pleased and elated with the uncertain life-style she now led. Sometimes they had hardly any audience at all, sometimes they seemed quite popular and well patronised. The members of the band called her their mascot. As for Tom, the nights they spent together, the music they played together, the way he put his arm round her when she felt upset, no one could have been kinder or treated her more tenderly. It all seemed so right somehow. The days passed happily, the nights were wonderful. She thought of Tom as her husband, even though they had not been properly married yet.

Spring came again. Tom decided they would not return to Blackpool for their usual season there, there might be too many complications he said, now that she had told him how old she really was. He didn't explain what he meant. They would stay on in Belgium he said. Time passed. September came, and then the cold of autumn and winter. Mollie didn't feel quite so comfortable anymore. Sometimes it was very cold, it was a particularly hard winter. Sadie gave her a large, warm but shapeless coat, in which she felt as if she might be drowning.

"It doesn't really matter what you look like," Sadie said, "as long as you keep the cold out. You can keep your hands warm inside those long sleeves." Mud and snow were everywhere. Christmas came and went. They all gave each other little cards, but there was no such thing as a Christmas goose or Christmas pudding, just another bottle of champagne. There was a dreariness about that Christmas. For the first time she felt a little homesick. She would have liked to have a letter from home, just to know what they were all doing. The winter seemed a long time passing.

As month followed month Mollie couldn't help but grow weary of the constant travelling and change. The excitement had somewhat worn off. She got tired. She didn't always feel so well. She never would complain, she had decided to live this way, and it was what she would always want to do. She wasn't ever going to admit to herself that things might be changing. She found herself unexpectedly weeping for no reason she could think of. It wasn't that everyone was not as kind as ever, but she felt herself growing apart from them, waiting, wanting she knew not what. She was restless, increasingly apprehensive, terrified if she would but admit it to herself, of what the next year would bring. She felt at times an intense loneliness, a great longing, but for what she didn't know.

Chapter 10
No Escape

Ruth was shaking Mollie.

"Wake up," she said, "I've come to take you to the hospital. Are you going like that or do you want to change?"

Mollie's thoughts slowly came back to Strangers Corner and the present. Remembering that other world of hers, those far away experiences she had never mentioned to a soul except Ned, and then only briefly, was foolish. She was thinking too much about the past, it was getting her confused. Ruth was now shaking her with some intensity.

"I've come to take you to the hospital," Ruth repeated more loudly. " Are you ready?"

"Don't shout, I can hear you perfectly well."

"I haven't that much time to spare, we can't stay long." Typical, thought Mollie, everyone is in such a hurry these days. She tried not to take too long getting ready, but there were the books she thought Ned might like, the letter he had received from his sister, the fruit and cake she had decided to take with her. She supposed she should brush her hair, but there didn't seem time. She would like to have changed her jacket but decided that would only irritate Ruth further. They went out to the car with Mollie feeling in a muddle, and Ruth trying not to show her irritation.

But of course, when they got to the hospital, Mollie was only too glad to have Ruth there with her. It was so difficult to talk to Ned these days, he seemed to have so little to say, so little energy to make an effort. She bullied him, she knew she did, but that had been her way. Those little moods of depression of his, even when they had both been young, meant they had to be bullied out of him. She had to support him, nag at him, get him to do things when he was in one of those negative moods. She quite understood when doctors talked about something called manic depression - euphoria one minute, depression the next. Not that Ned was very much like that, but he might be a bit despondent one minute, then become very enthusiastic about something the next. That was one of the things she always liked about him, his boyish enthusiasm for new things, new ideas. She could never have married someone who just liked dull routine.

Now she felt the weight of his current depression she wanted to bully him into a more optimistic mood, force him to make an effort to help himself. Despite the fact she knew he was not responding to her efforts, she had to try. Besides it was second nature to her now, she couldn't stop even if she wanted to.

"I've brought you some books to read." He turned them over in his hands without apparent interest.

"There's this letter from your sister, shall I read it to you?"

"She never seems to have anything much to say."

"I've brought you these, some cake and fruit."

"You shouldn't have bothered. I don't seem to be hungry these days."

"How are you, feeling better?"

"I still can't walk, at least only a few steps."

"Of course you can walk it you try. If you'd only put your mind to it. You could probably come home tomorrow if only you would make the effort to try." Ned ignored her, or seemed to.

"Why don't you listen, why won't you take any notice of what I say, why don't you even try and make an effort?" Her voice became shriller in her efforts to rouse his will to recover.

Ruth was feeling more and more uncomfortable, she couldn't stand her mother's nagging voice, nor her father's obvious apathy.

"They were asking after you at the pub last night," she said. "They all wanted to know how the Major was." She knew her father liked to be called the Major. That was what his friends there called him. The title had always suited him.

"Who did you talk to?" asked Ned, showing some interest at last.

"It was John Richards who was there, and Gerald what's his name, and old Ted, oh, and lots of others whose names I don't know."

"What about Arnold?" Ruth shook her head. "Give them my

regards when you see them again." Ned obviously cared more about those acquaintances of his in the pub than he did about her, thought Mollie.

A bell rang. It was four o'clock and time for visitors to depart. It reminded Mollie of a bell rung at the end of a school lesson. She was glad the visit was over.

She was driven home in silence, and once there sank thankfully into her favourite armchair again. How could a chair be comforting, it was just like an old friend. She sat there in the gloom not bothering to get a cup of tea, nor even to put on the light. The hospital bell seemed to be ringing in her ears. She found herself thinking of the convent bells of her lost youth. She could almost hear the constant ringing, bells calling the nuns to prayer, bells calling girls to classes, bells ringing from the church, bells ringing for prayers, even the tinkling sound of the bell announcing the host at mass. Bells, bells bells, and more bells.

*

The loudest bell at the convent had been the one calling the girls to meals, calling them to march into the long convent refectory where they were served lunch each day. Mother Superior would sit at the head of the table, grace would be said, and the girls would be allowed to sit down and start their meal. The nuns were very strict. No talking in the corridors, no talking at meal-times. It was almost like being back at her aunt's school again. Except of course for the nuns' dark habits, and the strange customs and strange beliefs, she might just as well have been back there. Once again she found herself isolated and alone amidst a school population.

Mollie didn't eat much when she first arrived, she was still feeling too lost and miserable. She would gaze at the statue of St Ursula which stood looking down on them from the refectory wall above and wonder yet again how it had come about that she should find herself in an Ursuline convent finishing school for girls somewhere in Mons. She was still in Belgium, but the band, Tom, and everything to do with her great adventure seemed suddenly to have vanished as if they had never been. She had had a hard time, or so the nuns told her. She had been ill, and she couldn't - didn't want ever to remember anything about it. She must think of other things now they told her. There she was in the convent, still feeling so miserable after all the weeks she had been there, still not wanting to eat, still not being able to sleep, still feeling like crying most of the time. The nuns kept asking her who she was, where were her parents, how old was she, what was her address in England?

"You can call me Meg, and I don't want to go back to England," was all she would say.

Who had arranged for her to be in that convent, that was what she couldn't really make out. She had been in a village somewhere, lying on a trestle bed with an old Belgian woman looking down at her. She could remember her kind old face with its wrinkles, the white cap on her head, and the soothing voice, though she couldn't remember what words had been said. Mollie forced her mind back to picture herself lying there, gasping and crying, scarcely conscious of what was going on around her.

"Buvez cela," the old woman had said, offering Mollie a cup to drink from. She drank whatever was in it. She must have been given some kind of drug for it had fuddled her mind even more, made everything seem unreal. All that had happened seemed like some kind of horrible, scarcely remembered nightmare, not something that had really happened to her at all.

The band had been playing late one night in a small Belgian town, that part of her memory was clear enough. It had been raining when they all started walking back to their lodgings. Tom was holding her hand. Sadie said they must stop and rest as Mollie stumbled along beside her, feeling rather strange with pains in her stomach. Sadie had taken charge, said arrangements had been made. There was a short ride in a carriage and then they had stopped at that Belgian house and Mollie had been given a bed to lie on and that peculiar tasting drink.

Mollie had gone to sleep, a kind of waking sleep as that nightmare unfolded around her. Perhaps she had some kind of illness like typhoid she told herself later, everyone said it gave you terrible stomach pains. She had lost count of time lying there on the bed. She was given more of that strange drink, drifted in and out of consciousness. She hadn't wanted to remember anything about it. She had hardly been aware of where she was. For years she had tried to make herself forget all about it.

She supposed it must have been a few days later when the old woman helped her into her clothes again. Sadie and Tom and everyone else seemed to have vanished as if they had never been. When she asked where they were she only got a shake of the head in reply. Bewildered and still half drugged, Mollie then found herself in the company of a kindly-faced, black-clothed nun.

"Venez," the nun said, holding Mollie's arm, and pointing towards the entrance to a dark passage. Mollie obeyed. She didn't see what else she could do, it all seemed part of the continuing nightmare. The passage led underground, it was very dark, it was lit only by an occasional flare. Another nun appeared, and between them they hurried her along, until they reached a wider part of the passage, less dimly lit. Along the base of a whitewashed wall she could make out plaques on which names had been inscribed, Soeur Marie, Mére Matilda she read hurriedly as she was hastened along. This was a burial ground, Mollie suddenly realised. Were they going to bury her there as well? It was like those stories she had read of nuns being walled up and starved to death. Perhaps she was already dead.

She started to run back down the passage, in a complete panic, anything to escape from that terrifying place. But the nuns held her, smiled kindly and pointed her towards a worn spiral staircase, which led upwards to the daylight. Then she found herself standing on the stone floor of an ornate chapel, with a statue of the Virgin Mary staring down at her. Perhaps she really was dead and this was the entrance to heaven, or was it hell?

She supposed she must have fainted. The next thing she knew she was on a bed again, with a nun sitting by her side, proffering her a drink. At first Mollie would not take it, although she felt extremely thirsty. She didn't want anymore of that strange tasting medicine she had lately been given so much of. But at last, in desperation because of her thirst she took it, and found it to be plain cool water.

"You're to stay with us here at the convent school," the nun explained, "it has all been arranged for you." Even then Mollie had begun to wonder who had done all this arranging. Sadie and Tom she supposed.

"You've had a bad time, we must forget the past, and think only of the future," the nun said. She had a soothing kind voice. Mollie slept for what seemed like days after that. The nightmare gradually lessened. They told her she had become an enrolled pupil in their convent school .

Most of those nuns had been very kind to her, she had to give them that. Of course they were strict Catholics, but she found in some ways they were not quite what she might have expected. Convents, if she ever had occasion to think about them before, she imagined to be bleak cold buildings with black-enveloped unworldly nuns gliding soundlessly and rather surreptitiously through long and draughty corridors. She envisaged them spending most of their time on their knees, praying in a cold and draughty chapel, full of crosses and statues of the Virgin Mary. She imagined them praying for a world they probably knew very little about. The rules would be very strict. Nuns would be severely punished by the Mother Superior for trivial offences like coughing during a service, or forgetting to say their rosaries often enough. Her cousin Christine's father, had been very scathing about nuns. But in reality she soon discovered they knew far more about the world than you might imagine.

Ursuline Sisters had always been interested in the world, in education for women and in working for the poor, she was told when she became interested enough to enquire. Within the convent they were extraordinarily strict; when in contact with the outside world they were very understanding. When she compared their compassion for what they called poor sinners, for instance, with the narrow ideas of Christine's father she was most surprised. Roman Catholics certainly followed strange traditions and patterns of worship. But when it came to helping others they seemed to know enough of the ways of the world not to seem narrow-minded.

They had good reason to be very strict with all the girls, she supposed. So many of them seemed to be English, the daughters of Lords and Ladies, one was even the daughter of an Earl - why else would parents pay high fees to this well established finishing school if not to see their daughters grow up to be the kind of young ladies a Duke or Lord might eventually wish to marry - accomplished, well mannered, and docile. Pupils were always chaperoned. A harsh word from Mother Superior would produce tears from any of the girls. Courtesy at all times, no pushing or shoving or shouting, the girls were kept well under strict control. No one would dare answer back to a nun.

One rule Mollie did find absurd. She flouted it whenever she could. Fancy having to have a bath with that great shroud-like covering over you to prevent you seeing your own body. You would see it anyway every time you got undressed. Not that Mollie much enjoyed looking at her naked self. Parts of her seemed to have shrunk, and other parts to have expanded during what she thought of as her illness. She felt how ugly her body had become.

There were all those statues of Mary the Mother of God and St Ursula, held up as models of virtue. There were confessions and penances, all of which made Mollie feel uncomfortable. The nuns did indeed spend quite some time praying, they smelled of incense and it was certainly very cold in the chapel, especially at night. No wonder the nuns needed to wear those thick black garments, they would probably have frozen to death without them.

There was Sister Veronica - she would always remember Sister Veronica.

"You should tell us who you are, my dear, tell us about your family," Sister said coaxingly.

"I'm called Meg," was all Mollie would say, "and I have no family anymore." But Sister Veronica was someone you could talk to about other things, she didn't seem to mind what you said. Some of the other nuns would have been shocked if she had told them she didn't believe in God, that going to services was a waste of time, that if there were a God you couldn't shut Him up in a building like a church or chapel with statues in it. If God were anywhere He would be out there with the flowers and trees, in rivers and rocks, not in some gloomy man-made building, however ornate. Besides why ever should a God, if there were one, be the least interested in the paltry doings of human beings.

"If you try praying to God He will help you, Meg," Sister

Veronica insisted as Mollie sat tired and listless, the tears running down her face, "you can't tell till you try, can you? Let us pray together, shall we?" That made Mollie feel acutely uncomfortable. Prayers, if there were to be any, should always be strictly private.

"I don't believe in prayer," said Mollie wearily, "I tried that years ago and none of my prayers were ever answered."

"Perhaps you prayed for the wrong things."

"I don't think so," Mollie insisted.

"Perhaps your prayers were answered in a way that you didn't understand."

Well she supposed it was possible that - all those years ago, in what seemed like another world, she had been able to have fairy Marigold as a friend in answer to her childish prayers. But she didn't really think Marigold had anything to do with prayers, or with God.

"Why do you believe in God?" asked Mollie.

"Because," said Sister, "I can feel His presence, talk to Him in a sort of way. Faith you know comes from experience of His love."

"He doesn't love me then," said Mollie," "because I can't believe in Him."

"Then you are very unusual," said Sister, seemingly not in the least put out by such a statement, "most people throughout history have believed in a god of some kind or other."

"That doesn't prove a god exists," said Mollie.

"Nor does it prove He doesn't. We live in a beautiful world, I'm sure you agree, and it's very difficult to believe we all got here by mistake, by some strange chance. However, I don't think you should bother too much about such complicated questions for the time being. 'Which of you, by taking thought, can add one cubit to His stature' the Bible says. I wondered, however, since it seems to worry you so much if you might be interested in the history of religions, I've looked out some books for you."

So Mollie read about what Sister called 'The great religions of the world.'At least it was interesting. Mollie spent a lot of time reading the books Sister gave her, which of course included the Bible.

"Maybe it will help you to understand why Christianity is the only true religion," Sister said. "It has always seemed so to me, because it teaches us about Jesus, and his command that we love one another."

"I like the idea of Mother Earth," was all Mollie said at the end of the discussions. "Natural things like plants and animals sometimes seem much more important than human beings."

"Well then, perhaps helping other people may help you to help yourself," Sister said rather sadly.

"Why was I brought here to the convent?" Mollie wanted to know.

"You have a friend, a truly Christian young man, English like you, who insisted you should stay here and be cared for until it was discovered who you really are. You were travelling with members of a concert band, I understand, who were no longer able to care for you, and your benefactor didn't think it right for a nice young girl like you to be stranded all alone in a foreign country. You are very fortunate, Meg, to have a friend like that."

"But who is he?" she wanted to know.

"That I can't tell you. We hardly know him ourselves and to tell what we do know would be to break a sacred confidence." And that was all Sister would say.

Mollie was asked over and over again about her family, and what her parents' name might be. "Meg," she would always reply in the same way, "and I don't have any family. They're all dead." Well they were to her. She couldn't face going back to them, even should they want her to. Oh yes, they would probably be nice and understanding, but she knew in their hearts they would condemn her. Her parents would despair of her ever becoming a reasonable daughter, her brothers would dismiss her as being beyond acceptance as a sister and Aunt and Uncle, who had understood her so little, would probably refuse to have anything more to do with her at all. Even Fred and Cook would be too shocked to treat her as they used to. If she was ever foolish enough to say who she was it would mean she would have to go back to England and disgrace. It was better to stay here in the convent, as long as she could, or at least until she decided what she wanted to do next. She was always very careful not to give anything away about her family.

Mollie settled down again after a fashion. She got used to the convent and its ways. She learnt more music, read books in French and English, learnt to paint, acted in the convent dramas. She went to chapel services and on Sundays accompanied the other girls to the white gleaming town church, averting her eyes as she passed the intimidating façade of the ugly foundling hospital building opposite. She enjoyed walking two by two with the girls through the town, admiring its old buildings and she felt some comfort in staring at the railway station, in case, she thought, I want to run away again some day. Life was not exciting anymore, but she didn't mind that, not for the time being at least.

If she did feel uncomfortable still with the rituals of the Catholic religion, she learnt not to say so. Even when nuns could be seen kissing the feet of a stone statue, or the presence of a priest would seem to evoke a kind of worship from the nuns, she ignored it. When the twittering of the girls as they went off to confession resulted only in their repeating the same offences the very next day, she ignored that too. She had found in convent life, a temporary haven.

Chapter 11
Rejuvenation

She was woken by the sound of her quarrelling grandchildren, audible now outside in the garden. Stiff, with her old bones aching from the cold, feeling for all the world as if she had just got up from kneeling in the cold chapel with the convent girls, Mollie eventually struggled out of her favourite armchair where she had been sitting for far too long, and found her way up the steep stairs to her own bedroom. Her reminiscences were hardly interrupted as finding herself warm again in bed, her mind drifted back to the puzzle of her benefactor, the man who had paid for her stay at the convent all those years ago, the man she so desperately wanted to trace now.

Perhaps, she remembered thinking at the time, it had been the aristocratic English gentleman who had come to some of the concerts, and inquired about who she was; perhaps it had been the well-to-do young man who had once sent her a valentine card, and whom she had never seen again; perhaps it was one of those friends of Tom to whom she had been introduced, but it seemed very unlikely; perhaps it was that horrid little man who had followed her round for a while. He had been living in one of those lodgings at the same time the band was staying there. Perhaps - perhaps, but most likely it was none of these. Such ideas were just fantasies, she knew. But she could think of no one else who might have taken such trouble to see she was looked after during the time she was in Belgium.

Her mind was drifting back to those convent days again. She remembered the nuns' capacity to teach and to earn the respect of the hordes of girls who seemed to swirl ceaselessly around the corridors all day long. The control was quite remarkable. The girls were taught to be kind to each other and to those less fortunate than themselves. Quarrelling and spitefulness were severely reprimanded.

"Now Isabelle, it's no use protesting, you were heard remarking how slow poor Claudette is with her English studies. You will say an extra prayer tonight for her benefit, and spend half an hour of your free time tomorrow to help her with her pronunciation."

"Yes, Sister."

"Now Annette, you were very spiteful remarking on Felicity's spots, it's not her fault she is so afflicted. You will ask her pardon, and say three extra Hail Marys for her on Sunday."

"Yes Sister."

"I won't sit next to Odette, I don't like her, - she smells."

"Desirée, what a dreadful thing to say. Go and sit next to her now, and ask for forgiveness in your prayers tonight."

"Yes, Sister."

But at the same time she often overheard the nuns making remarks about each other.

"Sister Elizabeth was allowed to hold the surplice for Father Peter yesterday when it was clearly my turn."

Mollie rehearsed to herself what she considered might be a just punishment for such jealousy. 'Say two Ave Marias and apologise to Sister Elizabeth for harbouring such jealous thoughts.' After all, if the nuns could mete out reprimands to the girls why couldn't Mollie hand out reprimands to the nuns. What's sauce for the goose is sauce for the gander as her aunt would have said.

"Sister Veronica, I'll have to tell Mother Superior that you were late for chapel this morning - I saw you sneaking in." 'Tell - tale, tell-tale,' muttered Mollie to herself, what about charity to others? 'Sister, you will spend an hour extra at your prayers tonight to ask for forgiveness for such spitefulness.'

"Excuse me, Sister Dominique, I am to take the girls today for their walk. You took my turn twice last week. I'll make a complaint to Mother Superior." Sister Anne was always making complaints.

"Sister Anne, you should be pleased for Sister Dominique," muttered Mollie, under her breath, "Sister Anne, you'll now have to wait another four days for your turn to walk the girls." Mollie thought her imaginary punishments were quite lenient under the circumstances. Nuns, of all people, ought to practise what they taught.

Although it amused Mollie to listen to such trivialities, somehow it was comforting to know that even those who had decided to dedicate their lives to God could still behave like ordinary spiteful, sinful human beings.

But now that her health was improving, she was beginning to find that convent life could at times be very tedious and frustrating. Her need for some kind of sexual satisfaction was incessant. It became almost an intolerable burden. Her whole body would cry out for the gentle touch of Tom's hands, for the way he would stroke her hair, and then gradually move his hands down her body as she ached for his probing fingers. She needed someone to press against, needed to feel the hardening centre of his body as it pushed into hers. She yearned to feel him inside her, to feel once more the love embrace that melted two people into one. She had read somewhere of a deserted Queen, banished to a convent, who was given a whip with which to lash herself to still the craving for some release of sexual tension. She wondered if she asked the nuns for a whip for herself it might help to put those all consuming feelings under some kind of control.

The nuns who taught the girls about their developing bodies would explain that girls always felt the greatest love towards the man with whom they first lost their virginity.

"That's why it's so wrong for girls to be with a man before they are married, they need to be certain a man is serious about his love for her. Besides it's a woman's duty to see that if she has children they will be properly provided for."

"Boys," they were instructed, "boys on the other hand, however romantic they may feel, experience love in a much more shallow way, their physical appetites are usually superficial and easily satisfied. They are attracted, intrigued, passionate even, but only really love a woman in the true sense of the word, after a period of settled home life, and with children to care for." Sometimes Mollie thought they might be right.

"It's no good expecting men to be other than they are," Sister said, "and women should behave accordingly. Men and women have different natures and alway will have. Women forget that at their peril." Mollie wondered if Sister had been jilted before she had become a nun. Perhaps, Mollie thought, some of the nuns did know, about the loneliness of a lost love, the emptiness of a desertion. Probably that was why some of them had decided to become nuns in the first place.

Although the chapel crypt was a place where the girls were forbidden to go, Mollie's curiosity got the better of her after a while. Her initial fright when she first arrived there, as she had been hustled along the ancient passageway, and up the spiral staircase, had now changed to curiosity. She found the idea of those nuns buried far below intriguing. What secrets might be hidden down there in the crypt? Somehow she must go and have another look.

One day she managed to linger unnoticed after evening service, and retraced her steps down the ancient stairway into the gloom beneath. She thought she remembered the plaques where the nuns had been buried had dates on them, and she wanted to find out how long they had been down there. Her curiosity got the better of her.

It was certainly dark and gloomy. Although a flickering lantern hung from the white-washed ceiling, it was hard to read the words written on the tablets at the foot of the wall - Soeur Elizabeth - Soeur Catherine. She could not see the dates clearly, although one did appear to be 1196. It was eerie, cold and draughty, she could feel sudden cold currents of air moving round her. She shivered, and turned to go. It was such a gloomy place. She wished she hadn't come.

As she turned to go, she found a nun was looking straight at her. She might have known she would get caught doing something that the nuns had so expressly forbidden. The nun just stood there, looking at her. It wasn't any of the nuns she knew from the convent. Come to think of it, the nun's habit was not quite like theirs in any case. The eyes still looked straight at her, straight through her almost, strangely bright and penetrating. Mollie backed away. She began to feel there was something insubstantial about that nun, something strange about those eyes. She wasn't exactly frightened of the apparition, if that is what it was, just wary that this might be another of her strange experiences, that she might actually be looking at a ghost. Perhaps this was one of those long dead nuns buried beneath her feet. I'm imagining things, Mollie thought.

She heard a voice. It was difficult to know if the sound was in her own head, or whether it was the voice of the nun who seemed to be standing there.

"You will see the child again," the voice said, "but not until many years have passed." The last thing Mollie wanted, she thought at that moment, was to be reminded of her recent history.

The apparition, if that is what it was, seemed to vanish through the wall and Mollie found herself standing there once more alone. She had not been frightened, not exactly, she might have been seeing ghosts all her life for all the effect it had on her emotions. It just seemed natural to have seen that figure, as if she had been expecting her. It was quite predictable that the nun would vanish in the way she had. What a very strange thing to happen, not something anyone else would ever believe. But how she wished these strange out of the ordinary experiences would stop happening to her.

She crept carefully back up the stairs and thankfully reached her dormitory without being seen either by nuns or other pupils. She sat alone on her bed for quite some time before she felt she could join them again in the refectory.

Lonely as she was, Mollie at last found herself a real friend. At first all the girls seemed more or less alike. But there was one girl called Maureen who always seemed to be hungry. She was often teased - when the nuns were not in earshot - because she was so fat. She had large dark pleading eyes, like a hungry dog. At meal times whenever a plate of bread came her way, she would pass it conscientiously round the table.

"Will you have a piece of bread?" she would ask anxiously.

"No thank you, you have it," was the invariable answer, no one wanted to ignore those pleading eyes. Maureen would very soon have emptied the plate herself. Perhaps it was the effect of eating just one extra piece, but one day the girls all watched with fascination as first one then another button popped off the front of Maureen's blouse, and tinkled to the floor. But no one laughed. The buttons were picked up and returned. The nuns were watching.

Mollie couldn't help catching the look in another girl's eyes, Grace by name, and later, when they were walking together down the corridor to their next music lesson, they both exploded in laughter. Poor Maureen, you couldn't help but see the funny side. They laughed until the tears ran down their faces. It was as well that no nuns were watching. It was the first time, Mollie realised, that she had really laughed for what seemed like years. After that she and Grace did everything together.

But Mollie still refused to say who she was. Not even Grace knew her real name, nor the story of how she came to be at the convent.

"One day I'll tell you, Grace," Mollie promised, but not yet. Orphan Meg, Grace called her teasingly. Grace's family lived in the North of England, she said. In fact Mollie realised they might even know her uncle and aunt. You never could be too careful if you wanted to remain anonymous.

Chapter 12
Rescue

Mollie woke in the morning to the sound of Ruth's voice.

"I've brought you some breakfast," she said cheerfully, depositing a tray on the edge of the bed. "I'll be working this morning, remember? But someone will bring you over some lunch later on and I'll be here to take you to the hospital this afternoon." And with that she was gone.

It seemed a very long morning. Mollie visited the hens, walked round the garden, attempted some rather desultory weeding of the overgrown patch of earth by the front door. She got herself a cup of coffee. She tried to read a book. She switched on the television and then turned it off again in despair, there only seemed to be those irritating cowboy films to watch.

She was pleased to hear someone knocking at the front door. When she opened it there was a man standing on the doorstep, a complete stranger. Young and good-looking, he was holding a sheath of papers in his hand. For a moment her heart almost stopped beating. Perhaps it was news of him, perhaps it was him. It was only a momentary thought, a trick of her mind, because he would be old by now, not as she had often imagined him, young and in the prime of life.

The young man was trying to sell her an aerial photograph of the house. She didn't really want it, although it must be admitted it was interesting to see the house pictured from the air in the middle of the surrounding landscape. But the young man looked so crestfallen when she said no she didn't want it that she changed her mind. I'll buy it for Ned, she thought, he can have it with him in the hospital, to remind him of what home is like. It cost quite a lot too, she wouldn't tell him how much. If only he could come home. If only she wasn't so afraid of being left on her own.

She was sorry when the young man went. It would be several hours before Ruth came by to fetch her. She settled down in her chair again, and her mind inevitably drifted back into the past.

★

She felt restless, bored, uncertain of the future, just as she was now, after she had been about two years there in Belgium with the nuns. She would have soon to decide what she would do next. Sister Veronica said that the payments for her schooling were likely to be discontinued soon.

"We would gladly have you stay should you wish to take your vows, if you thought you could be happy here with us. We think with time you would become a good teacher. But you must think very carefully as to whether you feel you truly have a vocation." Mollie didn't need to think, she knew she could never be a nun. She was surprised it had ever been suggested.

She decided she would apply for a post as governess, somewhere in England. She was provided with advertisements from the English papers. She considered many posts, but then applied for none, she couldn't feel that any of them would suit her. She would hate to be a nurse, she decided. What else was there? She did want to go back to England now, that at least was clear.

She started dreaming about London and about Blackpool. Such vivid dreams, repeated and repeated many times over. She told herself that it was only wishful thinking, that subconsciously she wanted to be found, wanted to be fetched home. But in her heart she knew it was something more than that - they would come, sooner or later they would come, somehow she knew they would. Their faces had appeared, their voices had whispered to her in the night. They would come soon, she was certain. Perhaps they would even forgive her for the past.

So she wasn't surprised when a Belgian and an English policeman came one day to the convent. Mollie was sure they must have come to find her. The two men had been ushered into Mother

Superior's room and stayed for quite some time. Then they left, leaving much speculation and gossip behind them. Mollie smiled at the recollection. Had there been a burglary? Was one of the new novices not quite what she seemed? Had one of the girls run away? Had one of the nuns disappeared? The whole school was at a fever pitch of speculation. Mollie was in a state of acute apprehension herself. What if they were not looking for her, what if she never got back to England.

A few days later the police came back again. Mollie remembered it as a bright, sunny day. She was sent for, now she knew she was right. Nothing had as yet been said to her, of course. But it hardly came as a surprise to find there, in person, in Mother Superior's room, her uncle and aunt standing in front of her. She had known they would come. They looked exactly as she remembered them, Aunt Penelope in a flowery hat, her uncle with his bedside manners, looking as though he ought to have a stethoscope around his neck.

"Thank goodness we've found you at last," her uncle said, as she sort of fell into his surprised arms. "We've always felt so responsible for not taking better care of you. Now, now," he said uncomfortably, "don't cry." Mollie felt no need to protest, no urge to run or hide at his seeming coldness, as he pushed her gently away. She gave her aunt an experimental kiss. She knew she was glad they were there. She was grateful they had taken the trouble to come all that way to the convent in the hope that she might be found.

There was much exchanging of news. Her father and mother, her uncle told Mollie, had been distraught when she disappeared. We have all been searching for you, hoping for some clue, and despite all the disappointments we have never given up hope of finding you safe and sound at last.

"Do you realise what unhappiness and inconvenience you have caused everyone by running off like that. What do you suppose all our friends and neighbours thought of it? Not even a note to tell us where you were," Aunt scolded, more from relief than anger.

"Well, we've found her at last," her uncle said interrupting his wife. "They're all waiting for you in London, your parents, your brothers, everyone. We'll catch the next boat across the Channel and then take you home."

"We shall miss you, Mollie, my dear," Sister Veronica said with some emotion. "I'm glad to hear you are called Mollie and not Meg, I never did like that name."

It was never explained satisfactorily who had told her uncle where to look for her. A note had been sent to him, he said, it had no address, only a smudged Belgian postmark. There was no other indication of where it had come from.

"You will find your niece at an Ursuline convent near Mons," was all that it had said. The writing gave no clue, written as it was in capital letters. A man's hand probably, her uncle thought. When he got the note he had consulted the Belgian police and come to investigate as soon as he could.

"Perhaps someone recognised you, perhaps a member of the concert band wrote the note," her aunt suggested. It remained a mystery.

Mollie had felt so ill on her arrival at the convent that she couldn't really remember anything very clearly. The nuns still refused to tell her anything about her benefactor. Could it be that it was he who had written the note?

As they left the convent Mother Superior gave her uncle a letter to deliver to her parents. What it contained she was not told, either by the nuns before she left or by her parents when she got home. She could torment herself by guessing what it might say, but no one would actually tell her.

She put the whole thing out of her mind. Her stay in Belgium receded into the past, almost as if it had been only a dream. Except that she brought home with her the two favourite pictures she had painted while she was there. One of those marigold flowers, and one of a Belgian sun setting behind some trees. Perhaps now she could start being ordinary.

Chapter 13
Home Is Not Always Home

It was difficult to know why some places felt like home, but not others. When Mollie came home from Belgium her parents' house felt uncomfortable. It was like that at Strangers Corner now, when she came back from her visit to the hospital next day. It felt too clean and too tidy, not enough people to make it look inhabited. The house was losing its familiarity, becoming almost alien. Highly polished floors gleamed in the sun, there was no one to walk over them in muddy shoes anymore, or spill things as they were carried from one kitchen to another. Everything was in its appointed place, cushions plumped, not sat on, no papers strewn about, no dirty socks to pick up from the bathroom floor. No shirts to iron, only infrequent pairs of pyjamas to wash and take back to the hospital. It had become an empty place. It never seemed to echo before as it did now.

Sometimes Mollie would stare out of the kitchen window, watching for the local children who sometimes came to ask for a drink of lemonade. Not so many years ago an old damson tree stood out there, but it perished reluctantly over the last two years, sending up untidy patches of dark green shoots over the lawn. She missed that tree.

"Can I'ave a drink, Gra'ma?" asked two rather unkempt looking children as she stood staring at where the tree had been. Mollie was happy to oblige.

She hoped they would soon come again.

She was pleased when Mrs Brown the cleaning lady arrived, as she punctually did twice a week. But now Mollie was hard put to find enough for her to do. However, she was grateful for the company. The two of them lingered over a cup of coffee, chatting about their mutual acquaintances at the Women's Institute.

"They miss you, you know, now that you don't come to meetings anymore. It isn't nearly so much fun nowadays. No one gives reports like you used to do, about plays and things, we could almost feel we were watching them with you." Mollie smiled to herself. Many a time she had forgotten completely that she had been delegated to go and see a play to report upon it, and had merely read the critics in the paper and made up the rest. She had never been caught out.

She ought, she supposed, to tell Mrs Brown that it would be quite enough for her to come just once a week. But somehow she couldn't bring herself to the point of saying so.

She went through Ned's suits, and put them all aside to ask for them to be taken to the cleaner's next week. He will need them when he comes home she told herself, he was particular about having his suits cleaned. She thought of putting some of the curtains in the washing machine. Some of them did look a bit grubby now, but she couldn't trust herself to reach them down without risking a fall. There was no point in weeding the garden anymore, since there would be no one to look at it. The days seemed very long.

Every afternoon she went to the hospital. She got to know the friendly taxi driver who picked her up most days. She looked forward to his cheery 'and how are you today?' and 'how's the Major getting on?' Sometimes Ruth would drive her in herself.

"I've brought your pension money from the post office," Ruth would say, or "I've fetched that prescription for you from the chemist." Mollie didn't want the prescription. What was the point of taking sleeping tablets - she seemed to be accumulating a little pile of bottles on the bathroom shelf. Often Ruth would bring her a grocery order from the village shop.

"You have to eat something, you know," Ruth said.

"It's just a waste of money," Mollie would retort, "I'm never very hungry. Bread and cheese and a cup of tea is all I need to keep me going."

"Do you think that perhaps I should have a word with Mrs Brown, suggest she might come only once a week now?" Ruth asked. "Those floors are polished so often they are becoming really quite slippery. You'll fall one of these days if you are not careful. Besides, it would mean you would have a little more money if you didn't have to pay out quite so much to her."

Mollie was furious. Interfering again, just like Ruth. She supposed she meant well.

"And what should I need extra money for?" she demanded. If there was an objection to polishing the floors she'd find something else for Mrs Brown to do. But why shouldn't the floors be polished? They made the house look properly cared for. It was her house, after all, and if she chose to spend her pension that way, it was nothing to do with anyone else. Nonetheless, she was always grateful when Ruth drove her to the hospital, Ned would talk to Ruth.

When Mollie got home each day, she was glad to retreat once more into the past.

"A house is something you live in, not live for," she had once said after a visit to a house so immaculately clean that one hardly dared cross the floor, let alone sit down on the well-arranged sofa. Houses had to feel lived in, welcoming.

Her parents' house, when she returned from Belgium all those years ago, had soon seemed anything but welcoming.

★

"Welcome home," her parents said when she arrived back with her uncle and aunt after her long absence. "Welcome home." And a welcome it seemed at first, despite the strangeness she felt after having lived so long in that different Belgian world. There were hugs and kisses, even a few tears. Her uncle and aunt left for Blackpool next day.

"Come and stay with us soon," they said. "Besides, your brother Harold is all agog to hear about your adventures." They went, handing over the letter addressed to her father from the Mother Superior.

It was then that things changed. Next morning, after her father had read the letter, he summoned her for what he called a little talk. He was standing with his back to the fireplace. He wasn't angry, it seemed, just quiet, more unbelieving, pained.

"That a daughter of ours could behave so" he said, "my little Mollie, I would never have believed it of you. What a terrible tragedy you have brought on yourself, ruining your young life so soon. Running off with a married man like that. Well, you will always have a home here, we certainly wouldn't refuse you a home. You'd better find yourself some kind of training for a job. You will have to be content with that, since it'll be highly unlikely that anyone should want to marry you now."

"Why should anyone else ever find out?" Mollie asked belligerently. "Why shouldn't I get married if that's what I want?"

"It's the principle of the thing," said her father, "If any man should ever ask you to marry him, which I very much doubt, you would have to explain about your past. Marrying a man under false pretences would mean only unhappiness for all concerned, surely you can understand that."

"If ever I want to get married, which I very much doubt, I'll make up my own mind what I want to say. It is nothing to do with anyone but me." Mollie was angry now, and close to tears.

Her mother came into the room.

"You've had your little talk I see, dear," she said, "now I hope we can all forget about it."

"I partly blame you, Minnie," her father said in answer. "You were always putting ideas of independence into Mollie's head even when she was small. I've told you many times that all this talk about freedom and independence only leads to unhappiness. Those wild suffragette women friends of yours, for example, will do nothing but harm. Women are becoming unprincipled, even getting violent I am told. No good will ever come of it. A man can only be responsible for his wife, look after her properly, if she is willing to behave reasonably." Mollie had never known her father make so long a statement or be so forthright. She always remembered him as a quiet mild kind of man.

Her mother said nothing more until her father picked up his hat and gloves from the hall stand in a distinctly put-out way, and closed the front door loudly behind him as he went off to work.

"Your father has his principles," Banna said. "I expect he will forget about all this given time. You can see he doesn't approve at all of my interest in the suffragettes. Men don't seem to like the idea of a woman's independence one little bit. They have been brought up to think of their wives as respectable dependent women, gentle and mild and obedient, following the example of the Virgin Mary, I suppose. He thinks of you now as what he would call a fallen woman."

"I can certainly see he doesn't approve of your interest in the suffragettes and votes for women. Will you still go to their meetings?" Mollie asked.

"Of course," she answered. "But I shall avoid getting chained to railings, or getting arrested, so he won't have anything like that to worry about."

Mollie soon found that she couldn't stand life at home, despite the longing she had sometimes felt towards it while she had been away. Her younger brothers were still away at school, her mother was often out at meetings, her father was still cold and distant. There was a cloud hanging over them all which made her feel acutely uncomfortable. She thought her father's censure would pass within a day or two, but it didn't. Her mother suggested she should go and stay for a while with her Aunt Fanny who lived somewhere in a remote part of Wales.

"You could see how you like the idea of nursing as a profession, your aunt seems to find it quite rewarding." Banna said. "Why don't you stay there until your father feels less upset," she suggested. Mollie readily agreed. She remembered her aunt from when she was young, someone jolly and kind, with whom she had shared jokes. Anything would be better than staying at home now.

Chapter 14
Uncomfortable Visits

They had arranged at the hospital for Ned to come home for the day.

"It'll be helpful for him to have a change of scenery," the doctor said, "help to lift him out of his depression. We'll see how he gets on. If this visit is a success, he might be able to come home for longer periods, two to three days at a time perhaps."

Mollie was pleased, they must think his condition was improving. She started to plan to make his visit as comfortable as possible. She was up early, and picked some flowers from the garden to put on the table. At first she thought she would ask Ruth to get some sausages, that was one of the things Ned had always liked best for lunch. There would be potatoes and cabbage available from the garden. She could provide a better meal for him than the rather indifferent hospital food she had sometimes seen left about on some of the patients' plates there. But then perhaps he might find that too much for him, better to have some eggs. She could make a quick curry with one of those tins if that is what he would prefer.

A car arrived at the gate, a wheelchair was produced for Ned to sit in, and he was deposited in the living room by the attendant driver. He looked bewildered at first.

"You can try walking a little later on, but you'll have to be very careful," the attendant suggested before he left. Mollie asked Ned about lunch.

"Oh, anything," he said, not bothering. "I don't eat much these days." He certainly looked a lot thinner than she remembered. Mollie cooked some boiled eggs which he hardly touched.

"Would you like me to push you round the garden?" she asked later. "Better not," he replied, "this chair will be much too heavy for you to push on your own." Mollie wished Ruth were here but it was one of her full working days.

"Would you like a game of scrabble?" So many evenings in the past they had played scrabble together, often into the early hours. He liked finding obscure words to use.

"Not really, I think I'll just look out of the window at the garden." The time seemed to be going slowly.

"Would you like to try walking a step or two?"

"I'm rather afraid of falling you see. You are not strong enough to help me as the nurses do." She couldn't deny that.

Mollie peered at the crossword at the back of the newspaper Ruth had provided earlier. She could just about read the clues.

"'Looking to the future', 'seven and seven,'" she asked hopefully. But neither of them seemed able to concentrate sufficiently to find the answer.

Fortunately there was a cowboy film to watch on the television. The time still went slowly. She made a cup of tea. They were both glad when he was taken back to the hospital. The change of scenery had not been such a good idea after all. After Ned had gone she just sat and stared sadly out of the window.

★

That visit to her Aunt Fanny in Wales, soon after she came home from Belgium, had been a very strange experience for Mollie. The journey there she remembered had become more and more interesting as she sat in the train watching the mountain scenery becoming ever wilder and more spectacular. Sometimes they passed by coal mines, with their ugly spoil heaps and strange smells. But then they would be out into the country again. And she had so enjoyed the last part of her journey in the pony and trap that had been sent to meet her. The sound of the pony's hooves drummed a welcoming tattoo on the stony road.

Her aunt and the friend she lived with - Mollie called her Aunt Annie - worked as rural district nurses, managing everything from midwifery to deaths. They provided simple drugs; supplied crisis nursing for various infectious diseases and gave sound advice to those with more routine complaints. Mollie soon found how very well-respected they both were. It was a remote area where little other medical assistance was available. How cheerful they seemed, how content with their simple life. They only seemed to need each other's company.

Who cared whether you lived half way up a mountainside - good exercise they said. Who cared whether the water had to be pumped out of the ground every time it was required - to some of the villagers a pump was a luxury, most supplies came from a bucket hauled up from a well, or taken straight from a running stream. Never mind that sanitation was a bucket or a hole in the ground. Who cared that the food supplied was so simple and so monotonous?

Of course there was gossip, it was explained to Mollie, there always was in remote places like this. "And vicious gossip it is at times," Aunt Fanny confided.

"Death by gossip, that's what it is," she said, indignation in her voice, as they discussed the recent death of a young girl who had pined away over the last few months. "She just couldn't face the tittle tattle. Not that she had given them much to gossip about, but once the village decides there is, you must either move away altogether, or spend the rest of your your life as an outcast. There aren't many can survive such pressure, however unjust it may be. So sad and unnecessary."

Mollie loved the high hills and valleys of Wales, the running streams, the clouds, the open space, the simple life. No wonder people said the valleys rang with song, even the scenery seemed to make music of its own. She was entranced by the beautiful voices she heard speaking that strange lilting language as she passed by the open doors of the various whitewashed cottages.

"Their songs are tales of heroes and magicians - it's a land of magic and dreams and legends. I only wish I understood the half of it" her aunt said.

There was a woman who lived by a spring high up on the mountainside. It was said she was a woman of sorrow, and that she had the gift of second sight.

The villagers were terrified of her. Unfounded suspicions and their malice had driven her to become an outcast, and they still feared her revenge. She was apt to make cryptic, forbidding announcements. They said she was to be avoided, she had made many an accurate forecast of impending tragedy.

"No one will go near that place," her aunt said, pointing up the mountainside to a cave in a rocky outcrop. "In my opinion she's just a harmless old woman, but everyone is scared of her."

One day during her ramblings Mollie found herself wandering over to those same rocks, and walking towards the cave where the woman supposedly lived. Curiosity had often been her undoing in the past. An old black crow sat there on a large boulder. A figure was bending over a fire in the cave entrance, the smoke swirling round her, blowing this way and that, so it was difficult to see whether she was old or young, pretty or ugly, but she was tall and striking in appearance, with long dark hair that obscured her features. It was a bit eerie, meeting her there, Mollie wasn't scared exactly, just intrigued. The woman was muttering to herself, the words must be in Welsh, Mollie guessed, because she couldn't understand any of the lilting lines.

As she listened, the words turned to English, and Mollie had no option then but to listen.

> Beware the world of sorrow,
> For death will come tomorrow
> Fear will rain down from the sky
> Arrows through water will fly.
> Ruins of earth with ghastly cry
> Woe to the days of tomorrow
> The burden of their sorrow.

Mollie shivered. She turned to go. No wonder the villagers were scared of her.

"Not so fast now, not so fast, my little lady," said a surprisingly gentle voice. "Come, sit down here beside me. Look in my eyes and see there the fate we all must share." Mollie looked, but quickly turned away, it was as if she were looking straight into pictures of hell, of struggling men and fire and blasted landscapes. How could you see something like that in someone's eyes?

"Sadness of heart you must bear, happiness too will be there," the woman intoned. Mollie felt she didn't have any choice but to stay and listen. The woman's beautiful eyes stared into hers again. She meekly obeyed, and sat down on a rock.

"Make the most of your days of pleasure, for soon will come the dark days of pain. But don't despair. You will know your desires in the lateness of time, for seven is your lucky number." The woman took her hand in hers and examined it closely.

"What is lost shall be found, as the years turn around. You'll see I am true in all I say."

Mollie had no idea what she could be talking about. She retrieved her hand, as the strange tingling feeling she felt in her hand subsided. She was relieved to be able to hurry away. What a strange woman. Perhaps, Mollie thought, she ought to have crossed her palm with silver or something, wasn't that the proper thing to do with fortune-tellers, to avoid bad luck? But since she had no money on her she just thanked her and said goodbye. When she glanced back the woman had gone.

An old crow still perched there on the rock, flapping its wings, and its cawing notes sounded just like 'beware beware.' Stop imagining things, Mollie said severely to herself. Then the crow too was gone as it flapped its way up the mountainside. She never mentioned meeting the strange woman to her aunt. But it had somehow made her visit to Wales seem forbidding. Like the villagers, she had become afraid of the strange woman on the hill.

Mollie was becoming wary of the strange experiences that seemed to follow her everywhere she went. Perhaps it was just her vivid imagination at work she comforted herself. But she didn't really think so.

Mollie had a letter.

My dear Mollie,

I have been considering going on a continental tour for the next few months. It is something I have always thought I would like to do. Your uncle thoroughly approves of the idea. He says that now his medical practice is so well established, I should take a long holiday, and stay as long as I wish. I need a companion to go with me, and so we thought of you. Could you let me know please as soon as you can when you would be able to join me. I do not imagine you will find it too difficult to make the necessary arrangements. Perhaps you would like to ask Grace, that nice friend of yours at the convent, to come with us.

Your affectionately,
Aunt Penelope.

Of course she would, Mollie thought, it was not a chance to be missed, she could always come back to Wales later on. Aunt Fanny thought it an excellent idea. Mollie replied immediately to say yes she would be delighted, and wrote to Grace asking if she could join them. She was quite glad to be on a train again.

Fred the butler, now dressed in a chauffeur's uniform, met her when she arrived at Blackpool station. He was driving her uncle's brand new car.

"Your uncle finds it a great convenience for me to take him on his rounds," Fred explained. That was a treat, to be driven to the house in an open car, with the wind blowing in her hair, the familiar landscape rushing by as they proceeded at what seemed the terrifying speed of over twenty miles an hour. Of course she had seen one or two of those horse-less carriages on the streets before, but this was her first experience of actually being driven along in one of them. Everyone seemed pleased to see her, and she them.

"Welcome home, Miss, me and Fred is so glad to see you back home again," said Cook with what looked like an attempt at a curtsy, but which almost ended in a fall. She had put on a lot of weight.

"Nice to see you back, Miss," Fred said, as he carried her bags up to her room.

Her uncle was as usual busy with his patients, but Aunt Penelope welcomed her as if she were a long lost daughter, with an enthusiastic embrace which almost knocked Mollie's hat off. Even her uncle and Harold greeted her with satisfaction when they came in after work.

She soon felt at home again. Of course when she had occasion to walk along by the pier and the concert hall she had to stifle thoughts that might have got her entangled with the past again, but she resolutely ignored them. It became easier and easier to pretend that the band had never existed, that Tom was only a character in a romantic novel she had once read many years ago.

To her surprise she felt much more at ease with her aunt than she ever felt in the past. She seemed more vivacious than Mollie remembered her, no longer having headaches and resting every afternoon. She was still her unpredictable self, one never knew from one moment to the next when she might change her plans. But somehow for the time being that only added to Mollie's feeling of exhilaration.

"Your uncle has found a wonderful new drug," she explained, "called aspirin. He prescribes it for all his patients now. I've only to take one or two pills for my headache to vanish." Her uncle seemed his remembered dour self, and was always busy working, saying he must attend to the needs of his patients. But even he was more forthcoming than he used to be for he had developed a new interest in collecting objects d'art.

"Everybody is doing it," he said, "no one is anybody these days unless they have a collection of some kind or other. We find pictures and pottery are what we are most interested in, don't we, my dear?" he said turning to his wife. He insisted on taking Mollie round the house to show off his latest acquisitions.

"Whistler, now there's an up and coming artist. What do you think of this print? How much do you think it's worth now?" Mollie shook her head. "At least twice what I paid for it, I should think," he said enthusiastically. As they went round the collection she noted the pride with which he stated each price, how he had found this bargain or that, how he could make a handsome profit on a particular picture, or wait for the price to go still higher.

"How would I know?" asked Mollie, "which things to choose? Why should anyone prefer one to another?"

"There are rules, one develops a kind of judgment," he said with self-satisfied importance. "Mind you, I don't go in for this new-fangled so-called art, not my style at all." Mollie had never known him so animated.

"Beauty is truth, truth beauty," Mollie murmured, quoting from Keats, "art for art's sake, isn't that more important than the money?"

"Of course some pictures give me more pleasure than others, but it's being able to understand the market, buy cheap, sell dear, guessing what artist will be next in favour, that kind of thing, that's what really matters." Philistine, thought Mollie, for a brief moment I thought he was actually interested in art.

That night as she stood at her bedroom window mysterious lights flashed to and fro across the sky. She wished she could paint it all, it would make a beautiful picture. Lights flashed and sparkled, and an ethereal glow shone across the dark sky. It was like a heavenly fireworks display. Why do these strange things always happen to me, Mollie thought, no one will ever believe me if I tell them what I've seen. Perhaps I'm dreaming again. But no ghosts or fairies appeared and the lights gradually faded. Next morning she was relieved to read in the paper that many thousands of people had also seen the strange lights.

"Some kind of atmospheric phenomenon that the scientists could probably explain - a meteorite perhaps landing in some remote part of Russia or North America," said her uncle. Aunt, who it transpired had also seen the lights, said it was so beautiful it must be a good omen for their projected tour. Fred and Cook said it was a bad omen, the forewarning of some kind of great catastrophe, like a famine or civil war, floods or violent storms. Harold said if that were so, he would make doubly sure to enjoy himself while he still could, and he couldn't see what all the fuss was about anyway.

Aunt Penelope's invitation to Grace to join them on the projected tour was accepted. Grace arrived, her usual bustling, interesting self. They caught up on all their news. She and Aunt Penelope seemed to get on very well together.

"I thought," said Grace a few days later, after the excitement and pleasure of her arrival had subsided a little, "that you said your aunt was almost impossible to live with."

"Well, she used to be, I ought to know," Mollie said feelingly. She was quite puzzled by the way her aunt seemed to have changed so much. The three of them, Aunt Penelope, Mollie and Grace went on shopping expeditions together - that at least hadn't changed - her aunt obviously still loved buying fashionable clothes. They had enough clothes, Mollie thought, to last a lifetime.

"I had another letter from Sister Veronica at the convent the other day," Grace said, showing it to Mollie. "You can see how interested she always is in you, wanting to know all about your whereabouts and what you are doing with yourself these days. She always did take a special interest in you."

Mollie read the letter, but in fact she wasn't really all that interested herself. She would always remember Sister Veronica with affection of course, she had always been so kind and helpful. But Mollie now needed to forget about Belgium, forget the convent, forget that she had ever left home. Grace seemed disappointed that she didn't take more interest, but the subject was dropped.

Mollie suspected her uncle was quite glad to see them go.

"Travel will help you to forget the past, Mollie," he said, "and your aunt, all of you, will find plenty to think about on your travels. We shall be very quiet here without you all, I'm afraid. Look after your aunt for me, won't you." Even her brother Harold condescended to wish them bon voyage. Fred and Cook gave Mollie a good luck charm.

"To bring you safely home again," they said.

Chapter 15
Travellers

So they set out on their erratic travels. Aunt was in her element, arranging things, ordering porters to take care of their luggage, demanding service, complaining if she were not satisfied with the accommodation or the food. Those were mad, wild unthinking times, rather like going for a very long ride on one of those Blackpool helter-skelters, all thrills and no substance, Mollie often thought in retrospect.

At first they travelled round England, visiting places like Bath and Harrogate. They would sometimes stay at the Ritz in London, with its marvellous electric lights, the exciting newly-invented elevator lifts which her aunt so much enjoyed riding upon, and its strange new telephone talking system. The lights were almost too bright, Mollie thought; going up in a lift was a distinctly odd sensation which she herself wasn't so sure about. As for the idea that anyone could actually talk to someone - hear their voice anytime of the day or night while they were still miles away - that was very intriguing. It was not the same of course as knowing what someone far away might be thinking - that could quite often happen in her experience. But using the telephone meant you could carry on a conversation with someone at a distance - now that was really very strange.

They went to London concerts, visited art galleries to buy pictures for her uncle, went to theatres, walked in Regent's Park and looked at the animals in the zoo, went to tea dances. Mollie loved dancing. She could always lose herself in the moving rhythm of the music.

"I could dance every night, all night, couldn't you?" she asked Grace. Grace just smiled as they took to the dance floor yet again.

Mollie liked fast waltzes best, and the dramatic movements of the tango. Even her aunt never seemed to lack partners. They had been provided with many letters of introduction, and soon they found themselves the centre of much attention.

"Your uncle has so many influential friends," Aunt Penelope said with great satisfaction, "his patients have always been so grateful to him."

It was a very exciting time for them all. Grace called it the champagne effect.

"Letting all the bubbles out" she said, "all those bubbles inside us we have been bottling up for far too long."

Then the three of them went further afield, on a protracted continental tour. Mollie called it their magpie holiday, snatching memories of this and that from here and there, collecting a motley of unconnected experiences, as they moved restlessly from one place to another.

"It's like going to the theatre," Grace said, "and being snatched away in the middle of every scene."

There was France, with its trains and wide plains, its rivers and waterways running through lush meadows, hills, vineyards and gentle warmth. There was Chartres Cathedral with its beautiful stained glass. They sat drinking coffee in the sun on warm café pavements, or indulged in long meals of many conversationally interrupted courses. A self-satisfied place, full of small towns with sandy central squares and smooth amorous young men. And Paris, of course there was Paris with its symmetrical streets, which felt itself to be the centre of the universe.

Here were German castles, fairy-tale yet menacing, perched on the edges of impossible high cliffs. The travellers floated down the great river Rhine, past the Lorelei rock and listened for the song of the siren that was supposed to lure sailors to their deaths. They drove through dark and sinister pine forests, followed in imagination by pursuing wolves or evil dwarves. They ate substantial heavy meals in dimly lit inns, they listened to heavy, solemn music and danced with stolid, polite young men.

They climbed the foothills of the Alps, the tinkling sound of cowbells following them as they explored the melted meadows with their profusion of surprising and delightful spring flowers. They stared at snowcapped mountains, shining in the sun. They breathed in the icy air, and wished they had wings to fly to those ragged icy pinnacles that shouted freedom at the skies. They crossed great lakes in little boats. They travelled roads that vanished into a neverending haze of distant blue, as if the pathways of the world could never end. Sometimes they travelled on strange little trains whose tracks clung to the rock faces of a precipice and felt as if they might fall off at any moment and plunge into the steep gorge below. Sometimes they walked patiently along stony mountain tracks to view the rainbows in a waterfall.

They visited picture galleries in Italy, felt the gentle light of the Venetian lagoon, and stood marvelling in the dim light of St Mark's Cathedral. There were canals, gondolas, bridges, water funerals and buildings that seemed to float on water. Aunt insisted on buying lots of lace, and colourful Venetian glass from the island of Murano. Sometimes Mollie and Grace were marched off to admire the interiors of cathedrals; they walked round gardens with fantastic fountains playing; they marvelled at statues and white stone buildings in the sun; they enjoyed visits to the opera. The Italian young men were very handsome. There were the ruins of Rome and the Vatican pictures. Rome somehow seemed sad. There was the Bay of Naples, Mount Vesuvius and Pompeii, and Aunt bought cameo brooches from men whose hands were disfigured in the making of them. They never stayed anywhere for very long - pushed ever onwards by Aunt Penelope's restless spirit.

They reached Austria, Vienna, and the exuberance of the Austrian Empire - great chandeliers of light in golden Austrian palaces, marble statues, lofty columns; great cathedrals with mosaic stone pictures glinting out their Christian messages. A grand panorama of the self - expression of a ruling élite, thought Mollie. For all that there was something decadent about it - too ornate - too glittering. It was as if the Austrian Empire was showing off, daring the Fates to punish it for its outward show of civic pride. It was an uneasy feeling, which she could not get Grace to understand.

By now Mollie was getting rather weary, the surfeit of travel and excitement was beginning to pall. A little peace and quiet would be welcome. Mollie felt she needed to go home to England. Grace was reluctant.

"I'm having too good a time to want to leave now. Everyone should make the most of opportunities, you never know if you'll ever get another chance like this again."

"All this travelling is giving me mental indigestion." Mollie explained to her aunt.

"We'll go home next week," her aunt announced in her unexpected way. "I am a little tired myself. But there are still a few things I would like to see before we leave." So it was that next day Mollie found herself standing in yet another cathedral, expected to admire yet another grand interior. She found herself on her own, Grace and Aunt had wandered off together, while Mollie stood admiring a Madonna with a lovely face.

As she stood there she had the strangest feeling, she could feel the hairs on the back of her neck prickling with alarm. She sensed someone approaching her, with some kind of intent. As she turned she saw that a tall, fair and slim young man, about her own age she guessed, or perhaps a little older, was standing there just behind her. She was sure she had seen him before, but where? In a crowd, in a cafe, who knows? He was with another man, also tall but dark, aristocratic-looking with a large nose and aloof expression.

"Miss Winder?" he queried. She nodded, somewhat confused. Why not Miss Allen? His companion nodded briefly, they both gave a slight bow. It was just then that a party of people pushed their way between them and herself, and when they had passed she saw that the two strange men were gone. She caught a glimpse of them hurrying out through the great cathedral door. She thought to follow them, but they disappeared so quickly she couldn't find them anywhere. She strolled in the sunshine, wandering outside by the buttresses of the great building, peering round corners, glancing along the various pathways. But it was to no avail.

She tried hard to recall where she might have met that fair tall man before, the other one she had no recollection of at all. She had met so many young men lately, it could have been any of several hundred she had come across on her travels. But this was different. There was something in the way he spoke to his companion, his tone of voice, his English accent, something in the tilt of his head, that made her think he might be some kind of ghost from her almost forgotten past. Why else should she have felt so perturbed? Mollie was mystified. Why should he have addressed her like that, called her by her aunt's surname, only to vanish immediately afterwards.

"There I go again," she said to Grace later, "I hate these strange happenings. Don't mention it to Aunt, she won't believe a word of it anyway." Grace could see Mollie was intrigued, perturbed even. Those two men obviously knew her, why else should they have accosted her in that strange way, then hurried off to avoid any further contact? Why could Mollie not remember who they were?

Next day Aunt decided to move on. Mollie would have liked to stay longer to satisfy her curiosity, go back to the cathedral perhaps, to see if those two men came again. But it was not to be. Her aunt had complained once too often to the manager of their hotel, and they had to leave hurriedly.

By the time they got back to England, Mollie could see how tired her aunt had suddenly become, exhausted in fact.

Chapter 16
Shadows From The Past

Ned didn't want to try another visit to Strangers Corner. But he could see Mollie was disappointed when they discussed it at her next hospital visit.

"Let's wait until I can move about a bit better," he suggested.

"I've brought some photographs to show you. I was looking through an old album, and I thought you might like to see some of them. Look at this," she invited. "We were so pleased with that snapshot you took, don't you remember, with the children all dressed in their sailor suits."

"Let's have a look," he said. It was the first time he had shown much interest in the family for quite some while.

"It wasn't easy, was it, bringing up those seven children? Harold had those terrible temper tantrums, don't you remember, when he would hold his breath until he went quite blue in the face?"

"I've often wondered," he answered, "whether I did the right thing in plunging him into a bucket of cold water every time he did it. I didn't know what else to do. At least it made him catch his breath again."

"Such fair hair he had. He was a good-looking little boy, wasn't he? When that picture was taken he had that sunny expression of his on his face."

"I remember we worried about them all, or most of them anyway. We thought Mary might be mentally retarded. Not a word she said until she was nearly three."

"She has certainly made up for it since. She's the only one of the girls to get a university degree," he said with some satisfaction.

"Here is one of Nancy - I can't think why she suddenly decided she wanted to be called Anne instead."

"Poor little thing, her eyes were so bad she could hardly see anything much until she was three when she had those glasses."

"She was always rather overweight after she was ill that time. But that hasn't stopped publishers in Canada wanting to publish a lot of her poems."

"Those temper tantrums of hers, she even ran away sometimes. She must have been about twelve the time I had to chase her across the fields one night to persuade her to come home again. She was dressed only in that flimsy torn nightdress of hers. Goodness knows what the neighbours must have thought."

"Thank goodness the social services were not around then. The three of them would probably be put into care these days."

"I slapped her, that's what I did. She calmed down and then said thank you, and came home as quiet as you like."

"They were an unruly lot."

"A bit of independence never did anyone any harm," he said.

"Just as well," she answered, "or we wouldn't have got married ourselves, would we?"

Marriage, why did people ever get married to a particular person she wondered? When she returned home she started asking herself over and over again, why Ned and not someone else?

★

"Now we are settled back home in Blackpool we must find a nice well-to-do husband for you Mollie," Aunt Penelope said half jokingly, when they returned from their travels abroad. "I had hoped you might have found someone suitable on our travels. But as our adopted daughter there should be no shortage of men wishing to marry you. You should settle down, have a family. I should like you to have a family. People respect your uncle, he is a man of substance now and he has promised to provide for you. And you know I have money of my own. Yes, we must definitely organise something. You must not get too much older before you decide to marry, or you'll find you have left it too late."

Mollie didn't care much for this idea, it made her seem like one of her uncle's objects d'art, to be valued and disposed of at a profit.

She felt aloof, indifferent, antagonistic even, to all the young men she had been so carefully introduced to by her aunt. She didn't wish to marry, not yet anyway she thought. She needed time to be sure the scars of her first love had finally healed. She certainly did not want to marry someone who had been chosen for her by someone else.

Her aunt became ever more critical of her; they had words. Mollie tried hopelessly to explain. Aunt Penelope said she was exhausted, her headaches returned. Mollie felt guilty, knowing she was probably the cause of all the trouble. Her aunt became even more erratic. Her uncle became more worried. He suggested perhaps Mollie should return to London for a while.

"She had set her heart on your getting married soon," he explained "and even started looking at patterns for wedding dresses for you. I shall have to employ someone else to look after her for a while. I think that's what she probably needs most just now." Mollie was glad to escape. She went back to London.

I am destined, Mollie decided, always to be a wanderer, a kind of outcast, never quite belonging anywhere I go. She wondered how she would be received, what her father would say.

She need not have worried, nothing concerning Belgium was ever mentioned. They listened with interest to her account of all the places she had been to visit abroad. It was a pity that many things had become confused in her mind - which cathedral belonged to which city? In which country was that particular view of snowcapped mountains? Which castle belonged to which German mountain side? Her parents must have found her account of her travels very sketchy. But she did her best.

"What a wonderful experience for you," her father said.

"I wish," said her mother, "I could have had such an opportunity as that when I was young."

Mollie decided never to mention her meeting with the two strange young men she had come across in the cathedral in Vienna. But she often thought about them.

She helped Banna file various accumulated committee papers which were scattered round the house. The suffragettes of course, and now the House of Good Hope devoted to helping unmarried mothers. There had always been her interest in various organisations devoted to promoting abstinence from alcohol consumption.

"I took the pledge," her mother explained, "when I was still at school - when someone came to talk to us about the evils of alcohol. It was a pledge never to consume alcohol in any form during my life-time. I've seen more misery created by men (and women too I'm ashamed to say) getting drunk and incapable and often violent, than from any other cause. So degrading for everyone."

Mollie thought of the parties she had enjoyed with Tom and the band. Some of the players had been drunk of course, but never violent. Drinking didn't inevitably lead to disaster. How dull and old-fashioned she found her parents now. Still it was better to have dull parents than no parents at all like her friend Grace, who was staying with her sister. She too had found life rather dull after all that travelling.

Mollie made a point of visiting her cousin Christine. Perhaps they could be friends again as they used to be when they were at school together all those years ago. Poor Christine had been persuaded by her parents to marry a clergyman of their acquaintance whom they considered a most suitable match for their daughter.

Poor innocent Christine, she had no idea what marriage was all about. She loathed her husband from their very first night together, and she had promptly fled back to her mother. She was terrified about her coming child, had resented the fact that she was pregnant. She was so changed, so unhappy, she now seemed destined to live the kind of lonely life more appropriate to an embittered spinster than a married woman, so wary had she become of men. She was so unlike the pretty spirited girl with whom Mollie used to have such fun. There seemed no point in their meeting again. Poor Christine, she would never know the pleasures of real love. Sex without love, that must be very difficult for any woman. At least I know what real love can be, Mollie thought, however unhappy I might have felt since then - however dull things seem just now.

Mollie received an interesting letter from her friend Grace.

Dear Mollie, fellow conspirator,

S O S, as the Morse code would have it. I don't know about you, but I am so very bored with life at present. I need to escape again from this dreary, humdrum life with my sister. I have a cousin who is going up to Cambridge. He is called Joe, and he has a friend called Danny I get on rather well with. He wants me to go and stay in lodgings there, says it will be fun. It won't cost too much, I promise you. Could you pay a half share do you think? I can't very well go on my own.

> *Do say yes.*
> *Your hopeful friend,*
> *Grace.*

Mollie wrote to say yes. She would manage it somehow. She appealed to her uncle for help. For all his remoteness, she had been so often grateful for his support. Her aunt's health was improving, he said. He was pleased to help, they would both be interested in the idea. It would complete her education, meeting young men with ideas of serious study. He had made some very good profits lately on his pictures. Celebrating by supporting her at Cambridge would please them both. He hadn't said so in so many words, but between the lines Mollie could read a renewed interest in the possibility of her getting married. So they they hadn't yet quite given up hope of arranging a suitable match for her.

They spent happy times together at Cambridge - Grace and her friend Danny, Mollie and Joe. Mollie liked Joe. He was tall and fair with blue eyes, handsome she thought. There was something - well nothing really - you had to get used to his manner, that was all. She supposed he had every right to feel rather pleased with himself. And there were all the other 'young people' (as her aunt insisted on calling them). They filled the streets of Cambridge with their bicycles, or strolled through the streets in droves, chattering and laughing together, as if they had not a care in the world.

In later years Mollie thought of this as her 'intellectual phase', 'mind travelling', 'dabbling in the abstractions of philosophy' - what people called becoming educated, she supposed.

Chapter 17
Cambridge

Cambridge was a friendly social kind of place, everyone agreed. There was picnicking on the grass along the College backs, the girls in their long slim skirts and high collars, daringly smoking cigarettes when no one was around to see, and sometimes drinking gin concealed in innocent looking teapots. There was boating on the river Cam, more concerts, more plays, more dancing. She and Grace had many admirers, and felt themselves sometimes to be at the centre of the social life of the university.

"Travelling abroad was all very well," Grace said, "but then I always felt I was on the outside looking in. Here I feel I am on the inside, looking out." Mollie knew exactly what she meant. It was exciting, flattering to be the centre of such attention. It was an intoxicating kind of life they led. A freedom to do and think whatever they might fancy.

Everyone talked, how they talked. Mollie listened. Sometimes she joined in. Mostly she found their conversations to be somewhat superficial. She delighted at times in teasing them, leading them on. They were very earnest, some of them. There didn't seem to be any subject that was not talked about at length at one time or another.

They discussed the Irish question, the monarchy, and the death of Edward V11 - a King who had probably, they said, prevented a new war in Europe by his friendship with the French. They imagined themselves at the Delhi Durbar in India, that glittering occasion when the Indian princes had done homage to their Emperor, the new king, George V. How right it was, they felt, that Englishmen should be destined to rule most of the world.

They expressed their fascination for unknown Africa - for explorers - missionaries - South African wars - Egypt and its monuments. They exchanged views on polar exploration and the tragic death of those on Scott's ill-fated expedition. They discussed the influence on art of China and Japan, along with the treacherousness only to be expected from all the inhabitants of that far Eastern world. Religion - politics - patriotism - and again the Irish question - philosophy - music - painting, sculpture, all came within the compass of their youthful enthusiasm.

They were fascinated by evil men, like the murderer Jack the Ripper. They protested against a world in which devastation was caused by natural disasters like earthquakes, droughts and fires and floods - all came under their scrutiny. How could a tragedy like the sinking of the liner Titanic, with all that loss of life, be allowed to happen? Why did people commit suicide, they wondered? That suffragette for instance who had been killed by throwing herself under the racing hooves of the King's horse, what had she hoped to gain by it?

What was the Fabian Society and why should the playwright Bernard Shaw be interested in it? Was there a need for medical insurance and pensions? Why was there poverty in the countryside, and how could the workers in the towns get better pay?

"You can help the urban poor by bringing in cheap grain from the Americas, and cheap frozen meat from the Argentine, but when you do, you ruin the farmers and the English countryside. You can't have it both ways," said someone, whose father was the owner of some large estate or other.

"What everyone must have is medical insurance and old age pensions. There wouldn't be much poverty if adequate provision was made for misfortune and old age."

"Don't you believe it," said Danny, "the Bible says 'the poor you will always have with you.' There will always be some people who are better off than others, and so it will be to the end of time. Give two people ten pounds each and very soon one will be rich and the other penniless."

"But no one should actually starve, or die of a preventable disease these days," said Joe, full of enthusiasm for his medical training and for recent discoveries in medical science. There was H G Wells and his science fiction ideas to talk about, new inventions, atoms, radio, flying machines, automobiles, transatlantic messages, moving pictures, man-made fibres, stainless steel, new chemicals.

"Just think what wonderful scientific advances are being made right now," Joe said with admiration.

"Wouldn't it be horrible," said Mollie, irritated by his self- satisfied optimism, "if all those science fiction ideas we read about turned out to be true? Those scientists, once they have an idea, they work at it until they make it come true, no matter what ordinary people think or want. Scientists don't just provide benefits for us all, you know, scientists never know when they have gone far enough. They treat all their experiments as if it were only a game they play, with no thought of the disasters that might follow. They would like that book 'The War of the Worlds' to come true just so they can play with their scientific inventions as if they were toys. It's likely that it will all end in the destruction of the world as we know it." Mollie liked stirring things up. Joe shouldn't be so pompous. Besides she was thinking of the sinister prophecy of the Welsh woman on the mountainside.

"My," said Joe. "You are a pessimist. Science is exciting, can't you see that? Practically anything will be possible in the future."

"I hope not," said Mollie.

"Women just don't understand these things, they should just stay at home and bring up their children, that's what women are really for," said someone else.

There was a pause, but Mollie let the challenge pass.

"You'll be telling us next that men will be able to explore the depths of the deepest oceans, or fly to the moon, or rockets will be dispatched to distant stars," Danny said, derisively. Everyone laughed.

"Now you really are exaggerating," Joe said.

"If there were another war, flying machines would drop things on people, and all those chemicals they keep producing will be used to kill people instead of helping them."

"There you go again, Mollie," said Joe. "Trying to put down science. You must admit it has its uses. What about the advances in medicine, for a start?"

"If everyone could be made to live for hundreds of years, just think what that would do to the world population. So many people would probably result in the destruction of the world itself."

"Now whose exaggerating?" said Grace.

"You shouldn't mock science like that," said someone.

" 'God is not mocked', you know, that's what the Bible says, there is bound to be a price to pay for everything. Probably the whole world will starve to death, or everyone will die of some new pestilence. The four horseman of the apocalypse will arrive, that's what all this science will eventually bring about - war, famine, pestilence and death." Danny said portentously. Everyone ignored him.

"There won't be anymore wars, fighting is out of date. There's no need for wars anymore, not in civilised countries like ours anyway."

"I for one don't trust all those politicians, they hardly ever make the right decisions," said Danny. "Science is like a machine out of control. You can't disinvent things once they have been discovered. And there will always be the unscrupulous, even the naive, who will want to play with fire."

"I think there may be some social law," said someone else, "like Newton's theory of dynamics - 'every action has an equal and opposite reaction.' How about 'Every advantageous use of a scientific discovery has an equal and opposite destructive reaction'."

"We have another pessimist do we?," Joe said irritably.

"That's why," said Danny, who had begun of late to take so much interest in the recent Roman Catholic conversions among the university students, "we need to renew our faith in Christianity, make people understand the will of God. Love is the only hope we have. If people don't learn to love one another, if we can't change people, then there is no hope at all, for evil men will soon have the means to destroy us all." Danny's interest in the Catholic church was much to Grace's discomfort, she resented the influence the priests seem to have had on him lately. He had become far too serious, she thought, and the conversation was getting out of hand.

"It's not that I think the ideas of Christianity are wrong, people should care for one another, of course they should," said Mollie, tongue in cheek again, "but all those solemn men - how they love to dress up in those embroidered gowns and things, and parade about in churches and vast cathedrals, feeling superior to women." Mollie was thinking of her convent days.

"You need psychoanalysing," said Joe, "who knows what strange ideas you have in that subconscious mind of yours."

"And that's another thing," said Mollie, "all that rubbish about sex and complexes delving into people's minds, and calling it a science. I think psychoanalysts like Freud are just stringing you all along, making a fortune out of people's willingness to believe some unproved theory or other. All that mumbo-jumbo, it doesn't really mean a thing."

"You are behind the times," said Joe, who by now was getting really irritated.

"I'm in front of them, not behind, you'll see," said Mollie. "But I suppose since men are so gullible about such things, it'll take years for them to see how they have been deceived. Science is becoming like a strange new secret religion." She was quite bothered by his uncritical acceptance of all things labelled scientific. Joe, she thought, was very naive in many ways.

"If it's strange new religions you want to talk about," said someone else, "why not have a go at devil worship. You must have heard the talk about that peculiar man called Aleister Crowley. He is a madman of course, very interested in Celtic rights I gather. He talks about witchcraft, conjuring up the devil - all that sort of thing. He has a place for women too, as witches of course. It's said he organises them in covens, in twelves, with him as a thirteenth. He is supposed to have them dancing naked in the woods in a kind of ritual ecstasy, so he can have his wicked way with all of them. You should meet him, Danny, that might have more effect on us than all this solemn talk of Christian faith." The conversation was getting out of hand again. Mollie wondered to herself what poor Christine's father would think of such a devilish conversation.

"It's only Christianity that can help decide what is right and what is wrong," Danny continued obstinately. "You'll find that out for yourselves one day." Everyone had become rather tired of the conversation by then.

Mollie's brother Francis had come up to join them at Cambridge as a medical student, and had sometimes joined in the discussions.

"You two girls could enrol as students at Girton College," he suggested. "I'm sure Uncle Arthur would pay the fees for you Mollie, as he does mine, and it would please mother I'm sure. You would certainly brighten up the classes. You couldn't get a degree of course, but you could learn as much as we do." Mollie and Grace thought that a splendid idea. Grace said she would make inquiries.

There came a day when Joe asked Mollie to marry him. They were gliding lazily in a punt along the Cam. She remembered thinking how men looked dashing in their boaters, those impractical straw hats that so often got blown off into the water. She watched Joe gently punting the boat along in his rhythmic athletic way. They stopped underneath an overhanging willow tree, where a little bird sat and sang. Why did it remind her so of that sad little Gilbert and Sullivan song of the lovelorn Tit Willow. 'Oh willow, tit willow, tit willow', she sang to herself, trailing her hand in the water.

He bent over and kissed her, as he had often done before. She felt comfortable in his big strong arms, protected. She had known he would ask her soon, and she had decided she would say yes. Of course she didn't feel the same about him as she had felt about Tom, how could she? She supposed you never felt the same about anyone else after you had once been well and truly in love. But he was kind, they had fun together, she wouldn't mind being a doctor's wife, and she was fond of him in a way. She was becoming amused rather than irritated by his pomposity. Perhaps she would really love him in time. She pictured their quiet family life together, something not to be forgone lightly.

It was only lately, very lately, that she had come to realise she didn't want to live on her own for the rest of her life. Fun and independence were all very well for a while, but she wanted something more solid than that. I am getting old, she thought, and no one may ever ask me to marry them again. Besides, now she had decided that what she most wanted was to settle down, because lately she had developed a longing to hold a new baby in her arms. It was that dream that had finally decided her, that dream she had so often lately, of herself stranded somewhere on a sea-shore, with the cry of a lost child carried toward her on the sea breeze. Search as she might in her dream, she could not find that wailing child. Wherever she might look - standing in the water - wandering along the shore - searching in the sand dunes, her frantic search was useless. She might think for a brief second she could see a tiny figure standing there, but then the vision would be gone. Sometimes just as the sound got clearer and she felt she might be about to clasp the child in her arms, the sound ceased, and there was only an uncanny lonely silence left hanging in the air.

It was odd, sometimes even during the day, she would look down at her arms, almost convinced that a child might be cradled in them there - a child with outstretched arms, rather like the Christ child statues she had grown used to at the convent. She had come to realise lately how desperately she now wanted to have children of her own to care for.

So she deliberately decided to become an ordinary wife and mother. Any marriage would be better than no marriage at all. Is it fair, she asked herself many times, to marry Joe just because she wanted children? But she would become a respectable middle class doctor's wife. She would know just what to do to help Joe in his career. After all she had spent all those years in her uncle's house and knew exactly what would be required of her. She would make him a good wife. They would probably disagree on many things, but she would just ignore his more childish ideas. Married life would soon cure him of that self-satisfied expression that sometimes irritated her. Those were the kind of thoughts that were floating through her mind, as the boat drifted along in the water. She would do her best to be a good wife, but it would be the children who really mattered. Why not, she thought, why not take this chance?

"Will you marry me?" he asked. She was almost startled, lost as she was in her own thoughts.

"Yes, you know I will," she answered, without the slightest hesitation, and he kissed her again. In fact he was kissing her for so long that she began to feel restless, and said it was chilly on the river and could they please go back now.

The engagement was announced, and everyone seemed pleased, especially her uncle and aunt.

'Your aunt is so much better, very excited at the news,' her uncle wrote. 'I hope you'll bring the young man to see us very soon.'

Her parents wrote and said guardedly that they must meet the young man, there was much to talk about.

'We can trust you I suppose', wrote her father, 'to tell Joe all about your escapade in Belgium.' Mollie ignored this. The past was no business but her own. It had nothing to do with the present, how could it have?

Everything seemed settled. Joe would buy a practice in Cambridge when he qualified. His father had promised to put up the money for a partnership there. Even the fact that she was a few years older than Joe didn't seem to matter. Joe would have his doctor's practice in Cambridge, Mollie would study English and music there at the university.

"At least until the children come along," Mollie said. Grace, who now announced her engagement to Danny, was to study French and English. It all seemed such a perfect arrangement for them. Mollie and Grace decided to go on a celebration picnic together.

Chapter 18
Dancing Flames

It had become the fashion in Cambridge to ride everywhere on bicycles, and to go exploring round the countryside. It was next best to boating on the Cam. Sometimes they would take a picnic. Mollie never told her mother that she went cycling, that she even sometimes wore bloomers, her mother would have been too shocked. Trousers of any kind were for men. It was unwomanly to
wear anything but a skirt, demeaning she would have said.

Mollie and Grace went off together on a long picnic ride and then got lost. They had been so busy talking of their plans that they hadn't noticed it was getting dark, nor that they had lost their way. This was somewhere they had never been before.

When they were cycling past some woods they saw the glow of a burning fire. At first it just seemed as if a bonfire had been left burning in among the trees - dangerous Mollie thought, the whole wood might be burnt down. Curiosity got the better of them. But when they ventured further in among the trees, shadowy figures were to be seen, moving in rhythm round the dancing, wavering flames of the fire. Too curious not to explore further, they moved nearer, and stood and watched in disbelief while it seemed that twelve shadowy naked women leapt and danced in and out of the flickering flames.

"Tell me I'm dreaming," said Grace, "it's all that student talk about devils and witches, we must be imagining it all. It's just shadows of branches swaying in the breeze, it must be."

Mollie was watching the shadows in rooted fascination. Grace nudged her arm.

"I'm frightened, it's weird, I'm off," Grace said firmly, "I'll not have anything to do with devil worship if that's what it is."

Mollie was still staring at the fiery circle.

"Come on," said Grace urgently, "I'll not wait." Mollie just stood there, as if transfixed. Grace rode off.

"Come on," she shouted over her shoulder as she rode away.

It was many hours later that Mollie limped back into Cambridge, pushing her damaged bicycle. Her hair was untidy, her clothes dishevelled with a tear in her skirt, her face blackened with smuts. She found Joe and Grace standing on the doorstep at their lodging house. They stared at her in utmost consternation. She must have looked a most strange sight, she realised.

"Whatever happened to you?" Joe asked aghast. "Have you been attacked or something? You look really awful. If anyone has touched you I'll...."

"No, nothing like that," said Mollie hastily, "don't be so dramatic. I must have fallen, stumbled over something, I don't remember much, I'll be all right when I've tidied myself up a bit."

"Come inside," said Grace hurriedly, "don't stand there on the doorstep for everyone to stare at you."

"Now," said Grace, as they went inside and Mollie sank gratefully into a chair, "tell us what really happened, while I bandage up this ankle of yours."

"I don't remember," said Mollie, "truly I don't. That's one of the strangest things about it. You went off, Grace, I remember that, while I was gazing at those weird figures dancing round that fire in the middle of the woods."

"They were just shadows from the trees," Grace said firmly. "It was very foolish of me to panic and leave you on your own like that."

"The next thing I remember clearly was lying on the ground," said Mollie, "with a painful bump on my head and a pain in my ankle. My bicycle was on its side a few yards away. The front wheel is a bit buckled but I managed to get back here somehow."

Mollie didn't know if what she had just said was strictly true. Perhaps, she thought confusedly, some strange power had drawn her into that dancing circle. In her mind she could still recall the twirling and leaping of the dancers as they gyrated in a kind of trance. Had she been part of that dance, she wondered, for how otherwise would her head be so full of the rhythm of their movements, the feel of the warmth of the flames, the magic of the shadowy figures? Or was it all imagination? She had lost all sense of time, of that she was certain. But what was real and what was a dream it was hard to be sure.

She had woken up in the dawn to find herself in the empty wood, not far from the burnt out embers of the fire. She had fallen, that was obvious. She had sprained her ankle and bumped her head and, she supposed, knocked herself out. Perhaps she had just dreamt about the leaping flames and the dancing figures. She must have fallen off her bike as she followed after Grace and hit her head as she fell, that was the likeliest explanation. She supposed she would never really know what happened.

Grace blamed herself.

"I should never have left you like that," she said contritely, "but I was really frightened. There was something very weird going on, you could feel it, you know. I thought you would be following me, but when I came back to look for you, you seemed to have vanished. I searched for you for quite a long time, believe you me, even though I was so scared," she said defensively. "There was no sign of you or your bike, nor of those fantastic dancing women. I thought I must have missed you and I should find you here when I got back. Danny and Joe have been out looking for you since first light. We have been so worried we were just thinking of sending out a police search party for you."

Of course, a great scandal followed.

"You are an idiot," said her brother Francis when he found out, "I can't think why you always have to make such dramatic gestures. You seem to make trouble wherever you go, it follows you round like some kind of curse."

Worst of all Joe broke off the engagement.

"How can I set up a medical practice in Cambridge as I intend to do, if my wife is known as a participant in God knows what kind of devilish orgies?" he demanded to know when he came round to break the news to her. "I can't have everyone saying my wife is a witch, now can I? You must see that. All my patients would very soon disappear." Mollie's protests of innocence were in vain.

"Besides, how do I know you don't have some kind of connection with that gang of necromancers?" She vehemently denied it, of course, but he only said that, true or false, such a scandal would be his undoing.

"I've always known there is something rather strange and fey about you Mollie," he said. "That's one of the things that makes you so attractive I suppose. But I can't risk the scandal, you do see that. My father is putting up the money for the practice and I can't let him down, now can I?"

"Since you care so much for respectability it's just as well that our engagement is broken off," Mollie said sarcastically. "It wouldn't do, would it, to get in the way of your career. I did wonder if perhaps your feelings for me were of a rather shallow kind. You say you don't want to marry me, well I'm telling you I don't want to marry you either. Nothing in fact would induce me to, now I know what kind of man you really are." And so they parted company.

Mollie never mentioned to anyone that she had found a strange book of spells in her pocket when she came home from her adventure in the wood. A few days later strange things began to appear in her room. She found a strange bunch of herbs lying on her bed; an envelope put under her door inviting her to join a witches' coven, another book of spells hidden under her pillow. I wonder, she thought, who it can be, someone up to some practical joke at my expense, I suppose. She didn't dare ask, in case something more sinister was going on.

Her uncle and aunt were much annoyed when she wrote to explain she had broken off the engagement.

'Such a nice young man', her aunt wrote, 'and so suitable. We were so pleased when you brought him here to meet us. All the trouble we have taken over you these last few years and you repay us by throwing away the best chance of a good marriage you will ever have. I can't make you out. What is it you really want? Your uncle and I've decided that we no longer wish to pay for you to stay on in Cambridge. From now on you'll have to make your own way in the world.' Stern words.

Mollie knew what that meant - Aunt had finally taken against her. Aunt was like that, on some imagined slight or other she would suddenly refuse to see someone ever again. She never relented, once she had made up her mind. Part of her strange personality, Mollie supposed. Her aunt frequently changed her mind about everything else, but not people. Mollie was really upset when her brother Harold wrote to say he had been told to have nothing further to do with her. Mollie fled back to London in consternation, taking those curious magic books with her because she didn't know quite what else to do with them.

Her parents didn't seem to mind that she had broken off her engagement. In fact they seemed a little relieved.

"Was it because of what you told him about your stay in Belgium?" her mother asked. "You promised us that you would tell him before you got married. You can't really blame him, can you?"

"We broke it off by mutual consent," she insisted. How could she explain to them the real reason why the decision had been made? It was best to say nothing. Her parents had received a cold letter from Aunt Penelope, saying they had no mind to see Mollie again.

"It'll be nice to have you home here with us," her mother said. "Francis will be home soon for his vacation from Cambridge and Arthur will be home for the school holidays as well. You'll be glad to see more of them I expect, especially Arthur. You'll soon settle down again in London, you'll see." The family seemed to accept that now she would remain there for good.

"Perhaps I shall turn into a sour old spinster. I shall become bitter like poor Christine, except of course she at least is entitled to be called Mrs, even if her marriage didn't last." Mollie was twenty four. It was most unlikely she would ever get married now. She would grow old and sour and ugly, looking after her parents.

She felt lost, humiliated. She begged her brother Francis not to say a word to her parents about the dancers in the wood, and to do him credit he never did. She played the piano to herself for hours on end; she secretly smoked a lot of cigarettes upstairs in her own room, taking care never to let her parents catch her doing so; she got thoroughly bored. She wrote frustrated letters to her friend Grace, who was now happily married and very enthusiastic about all that she was doing - she half-heartedly continued to help her mother sort out papers for her various committees.

She would have to find something to do. Perhaps she should go back to Mons. At least she might feel she was doing something worthwhile if she went back to the convent. They had once asked her to be a teacher. In the end she found herself a boring job in a local bank.

Chapter 19
New Beginnings

The first time Mollie saw Ned, her future husband, he was standing at the gate of his parents' house, scowling at the leaves on the path in front of him. He wore glasses. He had a broom in his hand and it was obvious he was supposed to be sweeping up the errant leaves as the wind blew them around. She was not quite sure why she should take note of him, even at this very first encounter. He was different, not like the fashionable young men she had met on her travels or at Cambridge. There was something about him that intrigued her, even if it were nothing else but a certain belligerence in his manner. Each time she passed his house on her way to and from the bank she looked again to see if he might be there.

She often heard the sound of music escaping as she passed by his house - a piano being played, a violin, an oboe, a clarinet. One day she heard the piano being played accompanied by the clarinet. She always listened to music, especially if it were of the non - heroic, intimate kind. Wagner was not for her, but Chopin, or Schubert, now those she would always listen to. This was Mozart's quintet in A. She just stood there listening, standing at the gate. The sounds became more ragged and disjointed as the music proceeded. There was an abrupt pause. A few heated words were exchanged but she was too far away to make out properly. Then that same scowling youth she had seen once before came abruptly out of the front door with a clarinet in his hand.

"I'm not playing with 'er again," he muttered to himself, as he walked down the path, oblivious it seemed to his surroundings. Then he saw Mollie standing there, and blushed. The two of them just stood there, staring. There was a long pause.

"It's no use," he said at last, "I just can't play with 'er - my sister - she doesn't understand the music. I can't keep up with 'er, she plays it much too fast."

Mollie noticed he spoke with a slight accent - not too pronounced but he definitely dropped his aitches. She found this quite attractive in a way. His voice and his manner proclaimed him to be what her father would call a rough diamond.

"Why don't you come and play at my house," she suggested on the spur of the moment, surprised at her own sudden decision to make such an offer. "We've a piano, and I know that piece quite well." She said it before she had considered what her parents might think of such an arrangement. Never mind, he would have to come round on evenings when she knew they would both be out. The young man seemed somewhat taken aback, and looked as if he might retreat back into the house at any moment He was still scowling.

"I've seen you walk past 'ere quite often," he blurted out, breaking the silence after a long pause.

"I'm Mollie," she announced, holding out her hand, "and you are?"

"'erbert," he answered disgustedly. "They call me Bert." He spoke as if he were ashamed of his own name, as well he might be, she thought. She nearly decided to cancel that invitation to play music at her house forthwith. Herbert, what an awful name! On what trivial matters can the future of people be decided. I can't get to know anyone called Bert, she was thinking. "Haven't you got another name I can call you by?"

He hesitated. He had always hated his name. It seemed to ring in his ears the whole time in the tones of his sisters' strident voices.

"Edward," he said uncertainly.

"Then I'll call you Ned," she announced, with such authority that that is what she had called him ever since.

Ned was soon to become a fairly regular if somewhat clandestine visitor to Mollie's house. They enjoyed playing music together, and the secrecy added a kind of excitement to their meetings. They laughed at the same kind of jokes. They respected each other. But as time went by, Mollie became more interested. She wanted to know about his family - were they really as horrible as Ned seemed to think? It was a long time, however, before she was invited to walk up that garden path and into the house. Ned had always seemed very reluctant to expose her to the inquisitive eyes of his family.

One day, after a great deal of persuasion, Ned did introduce her to them all. The first thing Mollie noticed was how difficult she found it to feel at home with them. There was a kind of antagonism directed towards her from the very first encounter. Not that they were not always pleasant and polite to her, it was just that an undefinable current of animosity seemed to prevail. She could neither understand it nor overcome it however hard she tried. Perhaps they didn't like her red hair, perhaps they were suspicious of her, perhaps they thought her not serious enough to be welcomed into their educationally dedicated household. She felt they were watching her to see at what point they could offer some new criticism. And they always seemed to be trying to put Ned down in front of her, which made her very angry. They talked endlessly about education, and achievement, and getting on in the world.

"All our boys have attended the Bluecoat public school," his father said proudly, "though I can't say Bert has made much of the opportunity."

"You realise Bert has no proper qualifications," said his mother, "he is going to find it difficult to support himself." Was she hinting that her son was no suitable match for a girl like her?

"Bert, you know, is the least musical member of the family. He does try, I'll give 'im that," said his father.

"Bert has always been a sulky boy," his mother explained. Perhaps this was another way of warning her off. Mind you, thought Mollie, he had a lot to be sulky about - a father who thought him very stupid - a mother who found him temperamentally difficult to handle - moody she called him - and brothers and sisters who seemed ready to bully him at every opportunity. She admired Ned for keeping his own end up despite everything.

Mollie could not help but have a grudging admiration for his father. He was a tall imposing man with a large moustache and very definite ideas about the behaviour of his family. He carried a watch, attached to his waistcoat pocket by a gold chain, which he often consulted. It was as if he begrudged the wasting of a single minute of the precious moments of his time. He was a barristers' clerk, self-educated. He left school at fourteen, and became a junior office boy at the law chambers where he was now employed as a senior clerk. He had taught himself to play the violin; he had read extensively; he had studied politics; he had become a respected member of the local community, and had been made governor of the local secondary school.

He had strong views on the need for the education of women, coupled with a strong emphasis on the courteous way women should be treated at all times. He was, she supposed, a pioneer of higher education for women. He was proud of the progress of most of his children, especially the girls. There were six of them, four boys and two girls, Ned was the third in line, after two older brothers, and next came the two sisters and a younger brother. His mother appeared gentle, but she also had her own strong views about the place of women in the home, and the respect due to herself as the organiser of the household. She got her own way as a rule, by gentle stealth rather than forthright command. She gained respect by her example. She took it for granted that her needs would be the first to be considered in any family discussion.

Ned was obviously thought of as the dunce of the family. His father, prompted by his sympathy for women, decreed that the two girls should be waited on by the boys, have their shoes cleaned, their books carried for them, doors opened for them, be escorted everywhere. The girls, Ann and Winifred, were supposed to help with the housework, but it was accepted that household jobs could always be delegated to the boys to allow the girls to study. The girls were supposed to work hard at school, they had brains their father said, and they should make use of them. George and Harold the older boys were supposed to be working too hard at school to bother with things at home, the youngest Lesley still too young to be made use of. The upshot was that their brother Bert seemed to have become the general skivvy, and the butt of much criticism and merriment. He felt, and was, the 'odd man out.' He resented being the one to dance attendance on the girls.

"I don't know how we managed to produce such a morose

kind of child," his mother complained, "none of the others are like that. I often wonder what will become of him. One minute he is all enthusiasm, the next he seems to be in the depth of depression. We hoped doing odd jobs around the house would take him out of himself." The sisters took full advantage of the situation you can be sure. Not a very happy kind of home life for Ned, Mollie reflected

It became apparent fairly soon that Ned's feelings for Mollie were becoming very intense. This increasing involvement rather worried her at first, it was such a responsibility she felt. Someone with such deep feelings made her feel wary. She knew it would not be long before he asked her to marry him. She was apprehensive, both excited and ambivalent about her own feelings. Had she really come to terms with her own past, she wondered? Would she be prepared to allow her feelings once again to become totally involved with someone else? She couldn't just marry Ned as she had planned to marry Joe. This time she would have to be totally committed, as once she had been with Tom. She could not be sure how she felt. Perhaps she should stop the friendship before further damage was done, although she realised things had probably gone too far for that already. Once or twice she nearly broached the subject, but found it too difficult. She could not bear to think of the look of betrayal she knew she would see on Ned's face were she to suggest that they parted. They seemed to have reached some kind of tacit understanding without Mollie quite realising it.

There had been rumours of war for years, but now they grew more ominous. There was unrest in Ireland; there was Germany's reported build up of its naval power. Politicians kept talking of their efforts to keep the peace, a sure sign of their apprehension that they might not be able to do so. There was discussion about the importance of the Russian and the French entente; there were questions in the House of Commons concerning the need for Britain to look to its defences. But no one really believed there would be an actual war.

"It won't come to that," Mollie's father said confidently, "it would be madness for Europeans to start fighting each other again. It would destroy civilisation as we know it."

The Archduke Ferdinand was assassinated in Sarajevo. Still no one believed the situation was that serious. The Austrians marched across the border. Everyone held their breath. Then the Germans marched on Belgium. Everyone knew then that it was war.

"It'll all be over in a matter of months," her father said confidently. "It can't last long."

Things seemed to change very quickly. There was an urgent need for recruitment. Posters appeared appealing to men to join up. A man and his wife, who had fled Belgium in fear of their lives, appeared shortly on the doorstep of her parents' house. They were carrying a suitcase which they said contained all their worldly possessions. They handed her father a letter from the convent where Mollie had once taken refuge. It was, they said, signed by the Mother Superior.

'These are people in fear of their lives, please do what you can for them. The situation here is desperate. Please tell Mollie he is safe. Please pray for us all.'

Her parents never asked Mollie who the 'he' in this cryptic message might be. Perhaps they guessed. Perhaps they already knew. Perhaps they preferred not to know.

So the Belgians stayed, grateful for any shelter offered. Their young daughter had been raped, they reported, and they had no idea where she was now. One of their sons had been killed. They had no idea where their other sons might be, they had simply disappeared. They had cousins who had been deported from their homes, and no one knew where they might be either. German soldiers, they said, were marching about the streets, laughing at the distress of the women they raped, at the fear in the faces of the children. Mollie's doubts about the need to go to war evaporated.

"War is always like that," Ned said. "Conquering soldiers always behave badly. You can't alter human nature."

Mollie and Ned decided to get married. "You never know what might happen in a war, we should be happy while we can," Ned said.

"We'll keep the engagement to ourselves for a while, don't you think?" Ned said. Mollie was in complete agreement.

It was not long after that Joe reappeared, dressed in a smart new army uniform.

"I've joined up," he explained, "like many of our friends. Doctors are urgently needed in France we are told. I have passed all my exams, but there is not much point now in starting up a medical practice in Cambridge."

Mollie wished him well. He fidgeted. Mollie wished he would go.

"I've come to ask you again if you'll marry me. I can't tell you how much I've missed you these last months."

Mollie was taken unawares. It was her turn to feel embarrassed. Yet she hesitated, as if there might still be a choice to be made. She rehearsed the old arguments - she was fond of Joe, and life would be comparatively easy if she accepted his renewed offer. She had always thought she would like to be a doctor's wife. He would be easy to get along with. Life with Joe would be placid, less intense, feelings would be less involved.

The argument stopped there. What was she thinking of? She compared him in her mind to Ned, and knew there could be only one answer. Besides she had a sudden picture in her mind of Ned's expression should she tell him she had changed her mind and was going to marry someone else instead. She couldn't do that to him.

"You're too late," she told Joe, "You shouldn't have been so quick to break off our engagement when we were in Cambridge. I'm already engaged to someone else, and we plan to marry very soon." She felt sorry for Joe, he looked so crestfallen.

"You'll find someone else easily enough," she told him. In fact he was married to some good-looking girl, she was told, a few weeks later.

Mollie introduced Ned to her parents, but thought it better to say nothing about the engagement.

"I hope you don't get too involved," her father said warningly, "not when there is your disgraceful past to be considered."

British soldiers marched about the streets of London. Posters appeared asking men to join up. Some men were sent white feathers because they didn't do so. Women gradually took the place of the men as they departed to the front. House servants left their employment to become postwomen, refuse collectors, bus drivers, munition workers in the factories. Women seemed capable of doing almost anything. Mollie worked harder at the bank.

German submarines started using torpedoes to sink ships. Some English citizens of German extraction had their shops looted. Mollie felt very sad about their local baker, such a nice kindly man, who was accused of being a spy. Mollie didn't believe it for a moment. One morning as she passed the bakery she saw an angry vociferous crowd shouting obscenities at the family, hurling bricks through the windows of the shop, helping themselves to the bread.

"Stop that," said Mollie, angrily to those nearby.

"So you're a spy too, are you," they shouted. "Look fellows, over here, here's another one working for those damned Germans." They started to jostle her where she stood almost crying on the pavement. There was nothing she could do but to retreat, and go in search of a policeman. But the damage was done. She often wondered later what had happened to that poor man and his family. They disappeared overnight, and were never seen again. She wasn't surprised to find that anyone with a German name now changed it to something more English sounding.

Ned joined up. He came back one day from the barracks where he was training, to say that since he might be sent overseas quite soon, he wanted to tell everyone about their engagement.

"We can call the banns and get married in a few weeks time," he explained to Mollie. He could see how happy she was. He went round to tell his parents, and she chose what she thought was a good moment to tell hers.

Chapter 20
Love And Marriage

Family antagonism exploded round them at the announcement.

"Ned and I are engaged, and we plan to marry in a few weeks' time. I don't suppose it can be much of a surprise to you," she remarked to her parents in an off-hand kind of way.

There was a pause, a long silence, not a word of congratulation.

"I assume you have told him and his parents about your past history, your 'escapade' in Belgium. It wouldn't be right to get married under false pretences."

"Whatever I did in Belgium is nobody's business but mine," protested Mollie. "I've been back in England for years now, and it's past history, a closed book."

"That's not our opinion. You must either break off the engagement or tell him everything."

"I'll do no such thing," said Mollie, angrily. "It's my business and no one else's."

"In that case I shall feel obliged to go round immediately to see his parents myself," her father said, "to tell them of your past behaviour - your running away to Belgium with that man, and all that followed. It would be quite unethical for you to get married without my doing so. Don't forget we still have that letter from the convent, given us when you first came home, telling us the whole story."

It was so unlike her usually mild father. How obstinate he was about Belgium.

"It's a matter of principle," he said, ignoring Mollie's protestations.

"Are you coming, Minnie?" he asked his wife. She hesitated.

"I'd better go with him, calm things down a bit," she said. Mollie refused to go with them. They departed.

Later Mollie received an account of her parents' reception at Ned's house. They had, Ned said, marched straight in and demanded a private interview with his parents. He didn't know what was said between them, for despite attempting to listen at the door (interrupted, of course by his curious sisters), he could make nothing out.

"I only know," he reported, "that they were closeted together for quite some while. When your father eventually left they demanded to see me."

"We forbid you to marry that girl," his father said abruptly. "We've been told about her past history, and she is not at all the kind of girl we would welcome into this family. We've always been worried by your apparent attachment to her. Now I see how very right we were."

"I don't care what her past history is," he told them angrily, "I'm marrying Mollie, and that's that. She's the girl I love - and that's an end to it." He marched out of the room, and out of the house. Then he had come straight round to see her.

They strolled hand in hand through the streets, avoiding both their own homes, talking of how they would get married as soon as possible.

"How dare they," Ned said, "how dare they dictate to me like that?"

"Do you want to know what happened in Belgium?" Mollie asked in some trepidation.

"Not really," he answered, "not unless you particularly want to talk about it yourself."

She decided to tell him about it, most of it, anyway. He was very sympathetic.

Ned went back to his barracks. Mollie spent the next three weeks uncomfortably at home.

In June 1915 they got married in a registry office.

"Much cheaper," Ned said cheerily, "and everyone is doing it now there is a war on." Ned was very understanding, considering he was in some ways a deeply religious kind of man. The only educational achievement he had was concerned with Bible studies. They rented a small flat with a piano in it. Ned was of necessity away quite a lot of the time, but that didn't spoil their happiness together. In some ways they were very glad not to have much contact with either of their families.

Of course, they had their quarrels, but they were too much in love to take much notice. Ned was a bit bewildered sometimes by Mollie's unexpected sense of fun.

"Have left and taken the piano with me," was a message he found awaiting him one day when he arrived back at the flat. They had words the night before, and he had to go back to barracks before they could make up. For an instant he felt he was drowning. But then he was greeted by peals of laughter as she emerged from hiding in the kitchen. All he could do was hug her in relief.

"Have gone prospecting, expect me when you see me," was another cryptic message that greeted him one day. Food had been getting scarcer. But she was back within an hour with some scarce commodity she had managed to acquire, hidden in her pocket.

"You'll never guess where I got this?" she said proudly.

"Where did you get it?"

"Stole it, of course." He wouldn't have put it past her, either.

She always kept him guessing.

Mollie's mother came to the flat one evening, unannounced. She seemed a bit flustered.

"Can I come in?"

"Of course."

"Nice little flat you've got." Her mother seemed ill at ease, as well she might.

"We like it. Will you have a cup of tea or something, now that you're here?" Mollie brought the tea.

"How are you both?"

"Very well, thank you. I'm expecting a baby, did you know?"

How could she have known, her mother thought, if Mollie hadn't bothered to tell her?

"Congratulations, that is good news." There was a pause. "I came because I was asked to bring you a message. Mind you I wasn't sure if it might not be better not to mention it. Your father said it might be best forgotten." Mollie imagined this would be some kind of conciliatory gesture from them both. Her mother took a deep breath and delivered the message in a kind of breathless rush.

"It's from a man, a Mr Hutchinson, rather a good-looking young man, said he met you in Vienna, in a cathedral. He seems to know a lot about you, through your friend Grace, he says, which is why he knew where to find us. Sounds a most unlikely story. He wanted to know your married name, I didn't see any harm in telling him that, but I didn't give him your address. He said he was in a hurry, had to go abroad immediately, something about the diplomatic service. He said to tell you you were not to worry, the boy was safe, and he would keep in touch with you when he could."

So that was the mysterious message. What had a Mr Hutchinson got to do with anything? She was as mystified as her mother.

"Thank you for bringing the message, but don't worry about it," she told her, "I'm in the dark as much as you are." Whoever Mr Hutchinson might be, she was grateful to him for having brought about a reconciliation between her and her parents. After that she found they got on better together even with her father. They both became quite fond of Ned and it was not long before Ned's parents were also persuaded to accept Mollie .

"I had to go and see them before I left for the front," Ned said. "After all it's just possible I might not be lucky enough to come back again."

Chapter 21
Wartime

The war proceeded. Her brother Harold was refused a call up until he had been treated for syphilis, the disgrace of which devastated his parents, and scandalised his uncle and aunt.

'Thank God it can be treated successfully these days with this new drug', her uncle wrote.

'I was just unlucky. I wasn't doing anything other than many of my friends,' Harold said in a letter of explanation to Mollie. They were all worried and anxious. It could be such a horrible long-lasting infection. What about the problem of possibly infecting his wife and children should he wish to marry? What kind of old age could he look forward to - shuffling around the streets - or worse in a state of derangement in a mental institution?

Uncle Arthur took charge of the nearby military hospital. Aunt organised the Lancashire Red Cross. She was in her element, at last she had found some real organising to do. Everyone did something. Mollie's mother ran a busy hostel for deserted and bereaved wives and unmarried mothers. There seemed an ever-increasing number of fatherless children to be cared for. When Danny joined up Grace went off to man a VAD post in France.

Danny was reported missing. There was the battle of the Marne. Ned went off to the front, came back on leave, went off again. There were mounting casualties. Food became scarcer. More ships were torpedoed. 'Arrows through water will fly' thought Mollie. A few bombs were dropped on London. 'Fear will rain down from the sky,' Mollie recited to herself. She had several miscarriages. There was the terrible loss of Australian and New Zealand lives at Gallipoli.

"Such a waste," her father said, "what a way to run a war."

Mollie felt very sad about the occupation and destruction of Mons. It was as if her own home town had been violated and destroyed. What was happening to the nuns, she wondered? She was especially anxious about Sister Veronica, who had been so very kind to her while she had been there at the convent.You heard such stories of nuns being raped and murdered. It was best not to think about it. It was said an angel had appeared to many of the allied soldiers - the so called 'Angel of Mons' to cheer them on their way. Mollie half believed it. Ned totally believed it.

"I didn't see the angel myself," he said, "But there were many men I know who say they did."

The Germans sank the liner Lusitania with about a hundred Americans on board.

"I wonder if the Germans realise what they have done. Now, sooner or later, the United States will have to join the Allies. At the moment they are too busy congratulating themselves on the advantages of the opening of their Panama Canal, but that will soon change now," Ned said.

News came of one terrible battle after another. Tales of the sufferings of soldiers in the trenches filtered through. Poison gas was used.Trains arrived back in London containing blinded men, crippled men, men with damaged lungs. They were met by sympathetic Red Cross volunteers. Lloyd George became prime minister.

Ned was awarded the Military Cross.

'For conspicuous gallantry and devotion to duty while his battery was being repeatedly bombed for four hours by enemy aeroplanes, setting fire to cartridges and causing many casualties. He personally took the lead in extinguishing fires and extricating the dead and wounded. He set a splendid example of energy and cool courage' said the citation. Mollie felt very proud of him.

"Others deserved medals far more than I did," was Ned's only comment.

The words and tunes of songs like 'Pack up your troubles in your old kit bag, and smile smile smile', 'Keep the home fires burning, while your heart is yearning', 'Mademoiselle from Armentiers,' resounded round the streets of Europe as soldiers marched along the roads bound for disembarkation. Some men came from overseas, with strange voices, strange faces, strange uniforms. The names of places like Verdun, Mons and 'Wipers' (Ypres) became common parlance. People became increasingly hungry. In Ireland some men were arrested for treason after a short uprising.

"Some bastards among them have been helping the Germans. They don't even care that they are stabbing some of their own countrymen in the back. There are plenty of very good patriotic Irish soldiers fighting for us in the trenches," said Ned.

You had to be inventive to make palatable meals out of the scant food supplies. Mollie once tried porridge with cheese - not a success. It was the only thing Ned had refused to eat that she ever provided. He usually liked her concoctions. There was no point in trying to follow recipes like those of Mrs Beeton, for example, as half the recommended ingredients would be unobtainable. People looked thinner, felt tired, and seemed to get ill more often. There were more casualties. There was little progress, despite various offensives. The whole country went numb.

There was a report of an intercepted telegram sent by a German official called Zimmerman, inviting Mexico to make war on the United States with German help. It wasn't long after that America declared war on Germany.

"About time too," muttered Ned. "We need them."

Mollie became pregnant again. Ned's brother Harold was killed in action. Francis, Mollie's brother received a bad gunshot wound to his head. A steel plate was inserted into the top of his skull where the bullet had penetrated. "It'll protect his brain from further damage," they said. "No one can guarantee that his mental capacity may not already be impaired."

Her own brother Harold was killed - 'Fighting bravely against great odds' said the notice. She knew when he was killed, perhaps the precise moment. She had woken sweating from some awful nightmare and she knew. She didn't know how she knew but she did. Some part of her self seemed to have got lost. Despite the awkwardness between them over the years, he had still been her favourite brother, the one who was so often in her thoughts.

"I think Harold has been killed," she told her mother.

"I don't believe it," she replied. "We've had no notification, how could you possibly know a thing like that? What a terrible thing to say!" Mollie hoped so much she was mistaken, especially since there was no confirmation for the next few weeks. But she wasn't wrong. The fateful telegram had been sent to Uncle Arthur, as he was Harold's adoptive father, and he had been away at the time on some urgent medical call. Three weeks passed before they knew.

Later came a letter, enclosing a faded red rose and a pair of lady's gloves that seemed to be the only personal possessions he had left behind.

"She was probably some nice girl he wanted to marry," her mother said through her tears. "I wish I could have known her. Such a pretty pair of gloves."

Poor, laughing Harold, the laughing soldier his friends had called him. That's how Mollie liked to remember him, how he had been described in the newspaper notice.

"Soldiers killed in battle go straight to heaven you know," said her mother.

Joe's name appeared in the casualty lists. Grace was reported missing and Mollie never did discover what happened to her. She thought she must be dead, she never wrote again. She just vanished, as if she had never been.

'Your country needs you' posters proliferated. The Germans advanced a little, were driven back; the allies advanced a little and were driven back. Would it never end? The endless list of deaths, the stream of maimed and shattered men arriving home. The Russian revolution took place. There were more problems in Ireland. The only good thing was that at the end of that dreadful year Mollie had a son, a healthy fair-haired boy, whom she named Harold after her dead brother. Ned, she discovered, was very good with children. How they both loved that first child of theirs. Not that it was very easy to look after an infant, there was the shortage of food, the constant disruption to their lives, the struggle to survive. Mollie breast-fed her baby for a whole year, to make sure he was properly fed. Then Ned was badly wounded.

Mollie went to see him in hospital. She was frantic with worry.

"Did you not notice, this is called the Hope ward?" he said in his weakened voice. "They've put me in here because I'm going to recover. It's a good luck sign. I'll survive, you'll see, you won't get rid of me that easily you know. It's a good omen," he said cheerfully. Then he fell asleep again.

"He was very lucky," the surgeon said, "if the shrapnel had been only a fraction of an inch nearer his heart, he would have been killed outright. As it is we've decided to leave part of the shrapnel where it is, it would probably kill him if we were to try and remove it now. Of course it may move at any time, and there is no knowing how soon that might be. But until then he'll probably be able to lead a perfectly normal life." Ned began to get stronger.

Chapter 22
Picking Up The Pieces

At last the Germans capitulated, the war was over. There were the wildest Armistice Day celebrations. The allies had won a great victory, so everyone said. But at what a cost! It soon became apparent that the aftermath of war was to be nearly as devastating as the war itself. Weary soldiers gradually began to return home from the front. The Belgian refugees went home to their shattered town but could find no news of their family. Everyone was exhausted. As if there hadn't been enough deaths already, a terrible flu epidemic swept the world, killing it seemed most of those who had survived the fighting.

"It feels as if the world will never recover," her mother said despondently. "Things can never feel the same again." Of course they couldn't. People had changed, everything had changed. "It was the end of an era," Ned said.

Wartime had been a time of numbness, a struggle for survival day by day. It was as if everyone had been holding their breath until it was over. When people began to breathe again, when the war had really stopped, and the wild relief of Armistice Day had passed, all that suffering and deprivation became locked up in people's minds, became confined to a kind of limbo, too painful to be recalled. When people began to breathe again the air they breathed was of a quite different kind.

Mollie gave birth to a baby girl. They called her Mary Hope. It was a difficult birth, a breech presentation, and she was born with a caul over her face which was snatched away just in time to save her.

"You needn't think," said Ned, "that just because the war is over things will be much easier. There will be quite a struggle for survival for the next few years."

For many life was far from easy. There was unemployment for

the returning soldiers, neglect or charity for the incapacitated. Earl Haig's poppy fund was initiated none too soon. Everyone was tired except the young. Young people in a wild reaction of relief, tried to dance away the past in restless exuberance. 'Anything goes' they sang, 'anything goes'. If you were rich you dashed about in cars and went to wild parties. If you were poor you went away to seaside holiday camps to have a good time.

Ned stayed on in the army as an officer in the accounting office, based at Aldershot. He, Mollie and the children settled in the nearby village of Church Crookham. Mollie found she liked village life, to live in the country was just what she needed.

There was a church service to mark the completion of the village war memorial, to which Mollie took the children, at her mother's request. It was a sad little Armistice ceremony, on a cold and blustery November 11th. People stood there in the cold, counting the cost of war, so many engraved names, so many homes with empty places, so many fatherless children, widowed wives.

> The sky is grey with drizzled rain,
> Red poppies lie.
> We stand beneath a stone-grey cross
> And wonder why.

> The wavering hymn notes slowly rise,
> Sad thoughts again.
> We see each others' downcast eyes
> And feel the pain.

> The vicar in his surplice stands
> As prayers are read.
> The cold wind gently swirls around,
> The leaves are dead.

> The empty names of unknown men
> Engraved in black,
> The sad and lonely list of those
> Who won't come back.

The clarion bugle sounds its notes
An eerie cry
To those who listen to its call,
For men must die.

Our sadness cries the sky above,
Why must they die?
We stand beneath this stone grey cross
And wonder why.

That was the last time Mollie went to an Armistice Day service. It was too sad.

They rented a little wooden house with a veranda. You reached it along a rough country lane, which took you through a fir-tree wood. It was like Hansel's and Gretel's cottage in the fairy story, Mollie thought. Little lizards sunned themselves on the silvery sandy soil, or scuttled off into the undergrowth, sometimes, if touched, they left their tails behind in fright. Bramble bushes were thick with autumn blackberries; bilberry bushes were everywhere. Nearby there was a shallow pond where frogs croaked and shy newts hid among the weeds. An occasional toad glared at her from beneath an upturned stone; rabbits came close to the house to nibble what grass they could find, and red squirrels played hide and seek up and down the trees. It was almost, Mollie felt, as if they were now stranded on a new and friendly island shore. Life was tranquil again at last.

She felt at home in the country. She had known she would, after that visit to her aunt in Wales. This is the life for me she decided. This is where, if I were the witch in the Hansel and Gretel fairy story, this is where I'd choose to live. Quiet! Peaceful! A simple rustic kind of life.

Despite the fact that Ned was still in uniform, the trauma of the war began gradually to recede. The feeling of numbness began to wear off a little. One needed peace and quiet to come to terms with the bad dream of those war years, and to refocus on a peaceful present.

The army provided Ned with an income while he worked to pass his accountancy exams. There were so many people out of work, a qualification was a vital necessity. The children could start their schooling at the famous army school in Aldershot run by a most excellent teacher called Miss Seed. Mollie had another baby girl. Ned rode about on his red motor bike, even managed to squeeze in the three children beside Mollie in the attached sidecar. They were provided with a batman - his name was Johnson - to help look after the house. Mollie loved it, living there in the country, almost in the middle of a wood. That was a good quiet time.

Ned began to lose his cockney accent, as Mollie helped him to speak what everyone called the King's English.

"You'll need to speak like a professional man, now you are to become one yourself," she said. He learnt a new vocabulary, as he talked to Mollie, and she explained the meaning of new words. He began to read more, especially history books. Ned was really quite clever, more original than most men were she realised. She was proud of him. All that energy of his, and he worked so hard.

She gradually felt her fear of being abandoned subside. Ned was always there to help with the children and with good advice if there were any crisis. He was someone you could rely upon. All she really wanted was Ned and the children.

Chapter 23
Paradise Lost

For a brief while Mollie felt quite content. The tragedies of the past were submerged in the present. She had her little children. She and Ned were in love, he could support her and she could help him. They lived in the country - theirs was an ordinary happy rural existence. It was some while, thankfully, since she had any of those somewhat strange experiences. They were just an ordinary happy family.

But, of course such tranquillity never lasts, there always has to be change - change and disillusion are in the nature of things. Living in the country could have its own hazards, Mollie soon learnt. There was a scare about the contamination of the water supply from the well at the bottom of the garden. Rubbish was difficult to dispose of, it had to be either buried or burnt. Sometimes there were heath fires nearby. Being isolated in the middle of a wood meant she met few people, made few friends.

Occasionally she wondered if some malevolent power followed her about, was she really responsible for bringing disasters upon herself? 'Trouble follows you around like some kind of curse' her brother Francis had once said. Perhaps he was right. It was certainly her own fault that one day their lovely bungalow nearly went up in flames. She had lit a bonfire to burn the rubbish, as she often had in the past.

Only a few days earlier she had been explaining to little Harold what a fire alarm was for, he was always asking questions about something or other.

"What's that for?" he asked.

"That post there you mean, with the glass at the top, that's a fire alarm. You smash the glass and that sets the alarm ringing, and a fire engine comes to put out the fire."

"Can I break the glass, to see if it works?"

"Most certainly not. People sometimes get sent to prison for doing that."

"Why?"

"It has only to be used when the fire brigade is really needed." By now the bonfire in the back garden was blazing merrily away. The children, throwing sticks at it to watch them burn, had been made to stand at a safe distance from the flames. Then there was a sudden gust of wind, swirling around as it changed its direction. Mollie grabbed the children just in time to pull them away as the flames flared into action. A nearby tree caught alight and was soon well and truly enveloped. The fire crackled its way rapidly through the neighbouring trees.

Panic-stricken, holding the children as best she could, Mollie ran as fast as possible down the road to the fire post. The excitement was much to Harold's delight. Mollie picked up a stone and smashed the glass, setting off the alarm. It wasn't long before the volunteer fire brigade arrived. The flames were put out, as water was pumped from the well at the bottom of the garden onto the blazing trees.

"Lucky we got here as soon as we did. It'll be safe to go back into the house now Missus," the fireman said in a kindly voice "me and me mates will be getting back to work on the farm now if you're sure you are all right."

"Fancy, all that fire from one match," said Harold's piping little voice. The fireman looked quizzically at Mollie, but shrugged his shoulders and made no comment. Wonderful people, firemen. Of course, Mollie felt guilty. She offered them money, but they wouldn't take it.

So it was that Mollie and Ned and the children had to leave their woodland retreat. Ned insisted. The wooden veranda of the house had been scorched, the house was now surrounded by blackened trees and scorched earth, and everything in the house seemed to be covered in black smuts.

"We can't live here anymore," Ned said firmly when he came home that evening, "too dangerous." Mollie didn't demur. For one thing it was quite impossible to keep clean, everything that was touched left a black smudge in its wake. For another the idea of the risk of another fire seemed too great a hazard to face. They decided to move out.

Samuel Allen, a kindly old man in his seventies, and a distant cousin, invited them to make a boat trip to his house on the island of Jersey for a short holiday.

"I heard about the fire," he wrote, "I think now maybe is the time for you all to have a change of scene before you settle down again. I've asked your parents to come too."

"You see how important it is," said Banna, "not to lose touch with one's relatives." It was a lovely seaside holiday, the first they ever had together.

Woodland Cottage was the name of their new house at Crookham. A nice name, Mollie thought, though a misnomer since there were few trees to bother about, for which she was really quite glad. The house was at the end of a little lane, with several houses round about. There were upstairs rooms, and a garden with a cherry tree in it. They decided to keep hens. There were neighbours nearby. Mollie made several friends.

Ned passed his accountancy examinations, in fact came second in all England. Mollie always thought he was clever. But his success brought changes too. It meant now he had to leave the army and find a civilian job. It was not all that easy, Ned was getting despondent looking for work.

Johnson, her friendly and devoted home help, had to leave.

"I'll never find anyone as good as he was," she lamented. "He was much more help than any woman would ever have been, such a handyman round the house." Mrs Jones, the new daily from the village, did her best. Helping in a house where there were three small children to look after wasn't easy.

John, her fourth child, was born soon after they had settled in. Her mother looked after the other children for a few days, and then came to stay and help for a week or two. Mollie had to confess that this time she was feeling rather tired after the birth of a new baby, and any help was welcome.

"If you hadn't been so foolish as to quarrel with your aunt you could have afforded a nanny to help you," her mother grumbled.

"I wouldn't employ one if I could," Mollie objected, "I prefer to bring my children up myself, thank you."

"I've decided," Ned said "to buy an accountancy partnership in London with someone called Lawson, who has been recommended to me. He has a practice in the city. It'll mean using up all our savings, I'm afraid. I'll be working in London but there is a good train service from near here, and it shouldn't be too difficult to manage the journey everyday."

Mollie, when she met him, didn't like Mr Lawson.

"He's too soft, too suave, too plausible. He'll have you doing all the work while he takes it easy," she warned him.

"What else can I do?" he said, "It's the best offer I'll get." And he did work hard, too hard. She was glad she had nearby neighbours since he spent much less time at home now. But at least he seemed to be earning good money.

He bought a car, a Sunbeam.

"The sidecar is too small for us now," he said. He certainly loved that new car of his, Mollie reflected, it was his pride and joy.

"Men are dotty about fast cars, I can't think why," she said to a neighbour, the widow of a retired Indian army colonel, whose husband had been knighted following the Indian mutiny. Everyone she met in Crookham seemed to have some connection or other with the Indian army.

"Men are all the same with machines, makes them feel superior with all that power under their feet," was the reply.

Mollie tried to learn to drive well, she managed to drive the children to school once or twice. But turning the car round was her nightmare. One day she backed into a ditch, and was trapped there for hours. Two young men in a very smart car eventually came to her rescue and towed her out.

"You know, do you, who those two young men were who pulled you out of the ditch yesterday? Only the Prince of Wales and his brother," said the neighbour.

"Whoever they were, they were very polite and helpful," Mollie said. She supposed they could have been the royals. She gave up driving altogether after that.

Mollie's Uncle Arthur died, the result of overwork during the war they said. She wrote to Aunt Penelope but got no answer. Her brother Francis got married to an American girl and they had a son. Her brother Arthur became qualified as an anaesthetist. Ned's brother George got married. Ned's parents died. The kind of changes to be expected, she supposed, in any family.

Sometimes at the weekend Ned would take them all for a trip in the car to the seaside - days spent on the windy sands at Wittering on the south coast - eating sand - contaminated sandwiches - trying unsuccessfully to dry children wet from the sea - drinking luke-warm tea from a flask - examining buckets with seaweed and crabs in them, while Ned built sand-castles for the children or let them bury him in the sand - in fact enjoying the primitive pleasures of the real seaside. Happy days.

The four small children were becoming a handful. They were always tumbling off the trees they were trying to climb or falling into the water, or getting lost. She was very glad of what she called her sixth sense at times like this. One time she caught a child as it fell over the banisters. She had decided for no particular reason that she ought to go out into the hall, and there was this bundle hurtling through the air, which she deftly caught as it fell. Another time as they walked along the canal bank, with Mary and Nancy trailing some way behind the pram she was pushing, she turned with a sudden apprehension.

"She nearly disappeared under the weeds in the water," Mary said, as her mother came hurrying back to see what might be the matter, "so I thought I better hold on to the last bit of her leg that I could still see." Mollie hurried the two dripping children home.

There was the time that a folding frame bed on which Mary slept had suddenly folded up over her head. Mollie went up to the bedroom in a state of panic, not knowing why, and extricated the almost suffocated child.

She was really worried when Nancy had a bad ear infection, and the doctor insisted on hanging up a sheet wrung out in some disinfectant fluid outside her bedroom door. The children crept about whispering in corners in case they might wake her up. The doctor wanted her to be sent to hospital.

"What nonsense," Mollie protested. "She's staying here. It

would kill her if you moved her away into some strange place with people she doesn't know."

"I suppose you were right," the doctor admitted, after Nancy had fully recovered. "There was another little girl the other day, she died, the move was too much for her. Home is the best place for small children."

Another girl, Ruth, was born - such a pretty healthy baby. Mollie so loved each new baby as it arrived. Children were at their best, she decided, when they were little helpless babies - a baby's smile, a baby's laugh, so rewarding somehow. And small babies stayed put in their cots.

Her parents came to stay. "Those children are running wild," her mother said, shocked as only she could be. "Their table manners are really dreadful. They don't even seem to know how to hold a knife and fork properly."

"Banna's cross again, and all because we knocked the milk over, and hid our crusts of bread on that ledge underneath the table top," they protested. "Why shouldn't we have friends under the table called Peddy and Gentules if we want to? We never stamped on Banna's feet, she just put them in the way." They were somewhat scared of their grandmother, but resentful too. Mollie rather dreaded these visits from her mother, they seemed to provoke the children's bad behaviour.

It was hard work keeping the peace between them all. Mollie was often tired. She missed Ned, who now frequently stayed overnight in London.

Chapter 24
London Unrest

All change again. It was decided to move to London, although Mollie at first vigorously protested.

"The children will need to go to good schools, especially the boys," Ned said. "They must go to a good public school if they are ever to get reasonable jobs later on." Even Mollie had to admit that the education available in the village school would be far from adequate. They were lively children, they needed to be kept fully occupied.

"Do you want all the children to grow up speaking with that horrible accent they pick up from the village children?" Banna asked.

"I'll be able to spend much more time at home," Ned emphasised, "no need anymore for all those train journeys. Besides, I shall be able to earn more, not so many wasted hours travelling about on those smelly trains."

"And it'll give you an opportunity to meet some of Ned's clients, wives can be such a help in that respect, you know," said her mother. Mollie thought of her aunt and the entertaining of her uncle's patients.

"I shan't have time to look after guests. Besides the children will probably have mumps or measles or something every time I arrange anything." Did no one realise just how tired she sometimes felt?

There seemed so many good reasons for moving that Mollie found it difficult to protest further. Woodland Cottage was vacated. Banna had undertaken to find them a house in Wandsworth Common, close to where she and Baba now lived.

"It'll be nice to have you and the children so near," said her father, who had recently retired.

"Besides," said her mother, "we are close to the Common, there will be plenty of room for the children to play."

So a house was rented. But what a house! Three stories and a basement. Whatever possessed her mother, Mollie complained, to imagine that the house she had chosen would suit them? She found herself forever running up and down those endless stairs. She was very uneasy about the stairs. She never lingered long at the top of the house, making beds for instance, it was too long a way down to the basement where the children played. More than usually uneasy one day, half way down, she heard a shout.

"Fire!" shrieked John's voice, "Fire!" There was an open coal fire in the basement, it was a cold day. She could hear him as she ran. "Fire, fire!" he shrieked. Anxious, agitated, and breathless from her precipitous descent down all those stairs she was met by Mary's calm gaze.

"The towel on the fire guard caught alight, so I threw it into the fire," she said. "I thought it was going to catch the fireplace alight. I hope you don't mind, but I didn't know what else to do." They moved out of the house to a more modern building the following week.

The new street they were in had gas lighting. Mollie quite enjoyed the lamp-lighter coming round every evening at dusk to light the street lamps. He made her feel safer when the fog came down, as it so often did in the winter, and the children came home from school enveloped in its wreathing clutches. She didn't have to worry so much that they might get lost.

It was an ugly modern kind of house, this one, no one could think otherwise. It was difficult to feel at home. But thankfully it only had one flight of stairs. Mollie soon began to hate living in London. She felt anonymous, lost, as if she didn't belong. But a prep school was found for Harold, and a 'ladies school' as Mollie labelled it, for the girls. The children found friends, and enemies too of course, quarrels had to be sorted out. There was a large area of open space of neglected allotments behind the house, where they could all play together out of harm's way.

Baba took the younger children for walks or played card games like bezique with the older ones. He had more time now. He had retired on quite a good income, thanks to the need for those wartime uniforms.

Soon after they settled in the new house in Ellerton Road, there was what the politicians called unrest among the workers. Unemployment rose, and some miners' wages were about to be cut. There was a general strike. London would be at a complete standstill. A revolution seemed to be imminent. People talked of the excesses of the French Revolution, and the more recent Russian atrocities perpetrated in the name of the workers. Mollie wished more than ever that she was not in London.

Volunteers were asked for to man the essential services. Mollie thought he quite enjoyed himself being a bus driver, when along with many of his city colleagues, Ned volunteered to keep services going until the general strike was over. He even seemed exhilarated rather than intimidated by the bricks thrown at him through the bus windows. There was a sense of camaraderie, as there had been during the war. People held their breath. The turmoil of revolution was in everyone's mind.

"The agitation will soon die down," Ned said. "It's sad, I have every sympathy for the miners, but they can't be paid with money their employers just don't have. The mines are running at a loss as it is. What they don't seem to understand is that if there is a revolution, everyone, particularly the workers, will find themselves so much worse off than they were before. They should read history. It's always the workers who suffer most after any revolution. I hope common sense prevails. Besides everyone is too loyal to the monarchy for such a catastrophe to come about in this country." He was right, of course, the strike seemed in the event to be but a minor irritation, as short-lived as it was ill-judged. No one could help feeling sorry for the workers. Improvements would have to be made somehow.

Money was becoming increasingly scarce and everyone seemed to be struggling to make ends meet. Ned found that supporting his five growing children was no easy task. Appetites increased; they kept growing out of their clothes, despite the use of reach-me-downs wherever possible. Schooling had to be paid for, uniforms provided, medical bills met. Life was now beginning to become a real struggle for survival.

"I've written to Penelope to ask if she can help you," her mother told Mollie, "but I didn't even get a reply. Now if your uncle were still alive, I'm sure he would have done something for you." How dare her mother, Mollie thought, go begging on her behalf behind her back, humiliating her. She could have told her it would do no good.

Down-and-out ex-service men, wearing wartime medals, came frequently to the door selling shoddy goods, grainy notepaper or imperfect household goods like tea cosies, or tea towels. Some begged for orders as they were on commission selling saucepans or new-fangled vacuum cleaners. Mollie hadn't the heart to turn them away, she could always find something to give them, however little. After all up to now she and Ned had survived the war shortages and the economic aftermath comparatively lightly. Everyone was short of money.

Buying poppies on Armistice Day salved the public conscience by enabling people to support those very badly disabled - those who could no longer look after themselves in anyway. But what of those Mollie called the 'in-betweens' the not too badly wounded, the shell-shocked or merely those with broken spirits and shattered lives? What was available to them? Many were too proud to accept charity, and begging was beneath them. Selling something meant at least they felt they retained some dignity. She always bought whatever she could. One of the callers stole a cigarette box once, it looked like silver although it wasn't. Good luck to him, she thought, but I'm afraid he will be very disappointed.

She tried to give up smoking, it had been such a solace during all those war years, but now she found she couldn't. The more she worried, the more she needed to have a cigarette, a kind of solace for London living, she supposed. It was an extravagance, but they cost very little after all.

Ned joined the Masonic Order.

"It's so useful to have as many contacts in business as possible," he explained. "Besides, I approve of their many charities, the way they look after their members, ex-servicemen a lot of them." Mollie suspected that the ritual and camaraderie were also to his liking, though he would never tell her what actually went on in those secret meetings of theirs. She was glad, since he worked so hard, that he had managed to find some form of congenial relaxation. Curious, she thought, that so many men like dressing up in fancy clothes. Perhaps it was because they needed a change from their dull city suits.

Mollie did entertain Ned's clients once or twice, though it was difficult with all the children to look after. She was always tired by the time evening came. In some ways it was nice to have other people to talk to, but it seemed such an effort.

One of the guests who came one evening, a Mason, was called Hutchinson. Mollie thought she might be imagining things again, she was convinced he was the same man she half recognised on her travels with her aunt in pre-war Vienna, the one who approached her in the Cathedral there. She tried to hide her confusion. She asked if he had ever met her mother. He shook his head. It was just her imagination she told herself. You wouldn't really be able to recognise someone after all that time, it was probably just some vague resemblance that had stirred her forgotten memories. Hutchinson, had she ever met someone called Hutchinson in her dim and distant past? He still looked familiar, but why she couldn't say. Perhaps it was his fair hair, the shape of his nose, his somewhat aristocratic kind of smile, who knows? He made her feel uncomfortable. If only she could remember where she thought she had first seen him. What could he ever have had to do with her? He gave no sign at all himself that he recognised her. Imagination, it must be.

Mollie wished to move back to the country, her parents wanted them to stay.

"Since you miss the country so much, I've arranged a holiday for us all at a small village called Mountain Ash," her mother announced one day. "I've made all the arrangements. If you can't live there, the next best thing is a country holiday." What a waste of money, Mollie complained to herself, I could think of a lot better things to do with it than waste it like this. Besides, I want to live in the country, not just visit it.

But a visit, she supposed, was better than nothing. She was glad her father seemed to enjoy it so much. He too was not fond of city life, despite the fact he had spent most of his life there. He was so pleased to be able he cut himself a smart new walking stick from a holly bush he found in the woods.

"Reminds me of my younger days," he said, "when us boys

stayed with my aunt at Alton and were free to roam the countryside. Now that would be a lovely place to stay," he said.

Mollie couldn't but enjoy being back in the countryside, despite her reservations. It gave her a feeling of relief and relaxation which she had missed ever since they moved back to London. The children relaxed too, helping themselves to the wild raspberries they found. Climbing trees again, searching for wild flowers, exclaiming over the appearance of rabbits and squirrels, beetles and butterflies, she realised how much they missed the country. But they didn't like the landlady much.

"She keeps complaining we make too much noise, and we think what she gives us to eat is horrible. Why can't we live in our own house in the country?"

Mollie made up her mind.

"Enough is enough," she said. "I insist we move back to the country, I'm not living in London any longer. The children are going to have a proper childhood. Children should be happy while they can, they need their freedom. Besides it'll be much cheaper to live in the country, you know," she said persuasively to Ned.

"What about schools?" he asked.

"The girls hate that expensive school they go to, and I don't think they are at all well taught. Mary can't even read yet, and she's eight years old. Harold has already got his scholarship to a public school now. We'll find schools somehow for the others." Nothing would make Mollie change her mind. In a way Ned agreed with her. Money and education were not everything.

Chapter 25
At Home Again In The Country

So they moved back to Church Crookham. Not to the same house of course, this one was called The Haven. It was cheap because it had been neglected by the previous owners. It was at the other end of the little lane from Woodland cottage where they had lived before. Some of their friends still lived in the nearby houses, it felt like coming home.

"We'll soon be able to make improvements to the house," Ned said. It was certainly old-fashioned compared to their house in London, but Mollie didn't really care. The house had a lot of small bedrooms in it, useful when so many children had to find rooms to sleep in. At the bottom of the garden was a disused stable for them to play in. There was room for a chicken run. There was an old-fashioned kitchen and scullery, with a tin roof over which the children frequently clambered. A large larder built on the north side kept the food cool, it had a zinc, mesh-covered meat-safe built out from its wall to catch the circulating air.

Mollie supposed she might miss some of the conveniences of a more modern house, but she found she didn't. Running a house like this, with five children to care for, was not easy, of course, yet it was a lot easier than in a town house for all that. For one thing the children could spend more time outdoors. They were always in and out, and there was no need to close the doors, let alone lock them. Everyone came and went as they chose.

They had a bathroom and a proper WC, the house had been modernised that much, Mollie was grateful for that. No main drainage of course. The coal-fired kitchen range heated a somewhat inadequate amount of hot water. On Friday bath night the children all followed one another into the tub. As they emerged they had, in winter time, to run the gauntlet - wrapped in a warm towel - of a freezing corridor, to reach the warmth of the sitting room where a big fire blazed in the tall old-fashioned fireplace. No nonsense about the sexes not knowing what each other looked like. There was a tall fire-guard with a brass rail round the top, to dry the washing on wet days or warm the towels for bath night. In the summer Mollie let them use it as a plaything, a pulpit for instance from which pretend sermons could be preached, or a castle wall defended from an Indian raid.

They had their own playroom, which she allowed them to decorate themselves. Never mind that part of the Japanese style wallpaper they chose, with its trees and bridges and little men was upside down in places, or that the paint ran in globules down the inside of the door. It was their room, where they did what they liked within reason, had their quarrels and patched them up, tried out their various games and skills.

For Mollie, cooking on the kitchen range meant learning the knack of putting one's hand inside the oven to test the temperature, and adjusting the amount of coal used according to the dish you might be cooking. Why was it, she wondered, that the food tasted so much better than it did when cooked on one of those modern gas cookers? True the range had to be black-leaded from time to time, but the children enjoyed doing such a messy job.

A built-in concrete copper with space for a fire to be lighted beneath it, stood in one corner of the scullery. Seemingly endless quantities of childrens' dirty cotton and linen clothing were washed - often boiled in it - to make sure that everything was clean and fresh. Mollie took great pride in seeing the children were properly turned out.

"They all look as if they have just come out of a band box," the new village lady help said with as much pride as if they were her own children. They could of course get as dirty as they liked in their rambles round the countryside, but she could always make sure clean clothes were available when needed.

Standing outside the kitchen door there was the old-fashioned mangle with its big wooden rollers. The children liked turning the handle to squeeze out surplus water from the washing, though Mollie often wrung some of it out by hand. Everything needed ironing of course. She heated her hand irons on the top of the kitchen range, spat on them to test the heat, cleaned them when necessary by rubbing them with a bar of soap. It was hard work admittedly, but worth it.

The downstairs rooms had gas lighting, which necessitated constant adjustment with the little chains that hung down each side of the globe shade.

There was the frequent changing of the little gas mantles which diffused a gentle light round the room. Candles were always used upstairs. The flickering light encouraged the children to imagine burglars under the bed, and lions and monsters in dark corners.

"Good for them to learn how to cope with their imaginary fears," Ned said.

Improvements to the house had to be postponed. The year they moved was the year of the Wall Street stock market crash. Now money really was short, as Ned struggled to keep his business afloat. Of course, Mollie was always over-spending the housekeeping money. If she and Ned quarrelled it was always over the problems of money. There were so many things to pay out for. She was grateful for any cheap help she could get in the house. It was Mrs Collis from a nearby council house who worked for her now - at low village wages - to keep the house at least vaguely clean. Her husband brought Mollie freshly picked mushrooms, or trapped rabbits, sometimes rhubarb from his council house garden, all at cut-down prices. Mrs Collis had a sister who was 'on the parish', supported by the poor law Guardians. With no other means of supporting her 'love child' as she called him, she seemed to manage all right, especially as so many people would help with such items as cast-off children's clothes. Sometimes her little boy came to play with Mollie's own children.

Each autumn Mollie took the children blackberrying, roaming over a vast open grassland called the camp fields. They could pick each visit about twenty pounds, and they all joined in the subsequent jam making. There was a muffin man who came round each week ringing his hand bell, with a tray balanced on his head, with muffins and cheap cakes for sale. You could always ask the village butcher for a bone or two, there was usually enough meat left on them to make a family stew, eked with potatoes and dumplings. You could save money by buying stale bread and broken biscuits at the village shop.

Practically all you needed could be bought in the village. There was a village butcher and a grocer shop. But best of all was 'Jesetts' at the other end of the village. Mr Jesett and his brother seemed to stock anything and everything. Mind you, you might be kept waiting for quite some time if your request was a little out of the ordinary, while one or other of them disappeared into a dark and cavernous back room, or mounted a precarious ladder into the shadowy attics above. But sure enough, patience always seemed to be rewarded. From shoe laces to long Johns, from pyjamas to a sun hat, from a selection of fancy ribbons or a choice of discreet flower-printed materials to a tin of beans or a locally cured ham, they would all be there somewhere.

Sometimes other things were needed like school uniforms. The first time Mollie went to the nearby shops in Reading which took an hour-long bus ride, she had one of those mysterious and perplexing experiences of hers. It was all to do with a dream she had, in which she found herself standing on a wide road in front of a tall building. There were a great many people standing around in front of it. Not that she would normally take much note of such a dream. But what was she to think of the fact that there in front of her, as she alighted from the bus, was that very same building she had dreamt of the night before. What possible connection could such a building have with her, she thought. But the puzzle for the time being anyway was quite insoluble. It was just one of those strange experiences that she would rather do without. "What's going on?" she asked a man at the door as she pushed her way through the crowd.

"Our Member of Parliament is coming to open an exhibition here," she was told. "If you wait by the library steps you may see him arrive in the next half hour." Mollie hadn't the time to spare, she would find it hard to get her shopping done before getting the bus home in an hour's time. She thought she caught a glimpse of that mysterious Mr. Hutchinson, but he was quickly swallowed up in the crowd. A pity though, if she could have stayed she might have found some clue as to why she had had that dream, what the connection might have been.There was always that feeling, just below the surface, of mysteries that might be solved if only she could find the vital clues.

The children too seemed sensitive to hidden things. There were sinister places in the village they wouldn't go near and always carefully avoided. One was the field opposite their house which belonged to a local farmer, and on which no satisfactory crop had ever been known to grow.

"It's where they buried them plague victims all them years ago," said Mrs Collis. "They covered all them corpses with quicklime, they did, and no crop has ever done any good since. Stands to reason. Much better leave it go for grass."

Another was a pond they found far into the woods.

"It's horrid there," Mary reported, coming back from one of their lengthy explorations one day. "All damp and dark, with straggly tumble down trees leaning down over some steep banks, and at the bottom a dark mysterious pool of black water. It feels as if an evil spirit is hiding there." She shivered. "I've said none of us is ever to go near it, or something horrible will happen, I know it will."

"That pond," said Mrs Collis, "they say is cursed. People get drowned there. Why a young lad was killed only a year or two ago. He fell in and could not get out, they said. Poor lad. There was a rumour too, some said it might not have been an accident after all, they say someone might have pushed him down there. But me, I never listen to such gossip."

Time moves on too fast, Mollie thought. Some family members had vanished into the past, like that little boy. Ned's parents had died, and his younger brother. Baba died. He had hiccoughs for a week and then died of pancreatic cancer. He was a good man. It was he, after all, whom Mollie had come to rely on when she came home from staying with her hated Aunt Ada. They all missed him. Ned could still shed tears at such bereavements.

Ned was always busy and often very tired, but he sometimes found time to take the family for days out on expeditions to the seaside. No matter it was so often cold and windy at Wittering on the south coast where they usually went. It was just miles and miles of sand and nothing else. All those picnics with gritty sand in the sandwiches, lukewarm tea from a thermos, and vain attempts to dry shivering children wet from the sea. But such treats got rarer.

"Things are even worse than usual, I've no money to pay the wages of my secretary, nor any money for next week's housekeeping," Ned said one day. "But I have every faith in the kindness of fortune. One of my clients who owes me money will pay up this week, you'll see." And sure enough he did. Ned had a lucky streak about him, his optimism always seemed to pay off. If he backed horses in a race, he always won, though he didn't try it very often.

"I bet only on the Grand National, or when I'm desperate," he said.

Schools had been sorted out. Harold took up his scholarship to a public school as a day boy, living with his uncle Francis and his American born wife in London. Mary went to a nearby grammar school which she hated. Nancy, John and Ruth were taught 'the three Rs' - reading, writing and arithmetic by a kindly and competent ex - teacher neighbour.

Mollie had long forgotten about those books of magic spells she had so mysteriously come by in Cambridge.

"We went up to the churchyard last night, me and Nancy and John," Mary announced one morning, "we got up in the middle of the night, it said we had to be there at midnight, and we tried to conjure up the devil. It's all in this book I found in the bookcase. Of course nothing happened," she continued in a disappointed voice. "Perhaps we got the spell wrong."

Mollie said "Oh yes" in a non-committal kind of way, but for once was a little startled. She forthwith removed any possible trace of magic references from the bookshelves. Ned said he thought that going to church for christenings was not enough, and from now on he would take the children to church every Sunday. He knew Mollie didn't like churches much herself. The subject of the devil never got mentioned again. None of the children much liked church.

Of course there were animals - hens fed on household scraps provided eggs. The children knew them all by names they had given them, and refused to eat any of their pets, should the time come when one or other had outlived its usefulness. There were cats, especially 'wonk-eye' the slightly deformed tabby. There was Pip the dog who disappeared one day, and whose skeleton and collar were found a year later when a badgers' set on the canal bank was being dug out. There were intermittent tame rabbits or guinea pigs in cages on the grass.

Harold, having been taught the names of many of the wild flowers, taught them to everyone else. The children told each other long and complicated stories.

They identified butterflies and moths; they climbed trees to inspect the contents of birds' nests to add yet another kind of egg to their collection. Once Mary half fell out of a high tree when surprised by the inhabiting owl which flew at her. They picked quantities of flowers to decorate the local church, especially primroses at Easter, each year the woods were crowded with them, you could not help but step on some of them. Each year there were wild daffodils in a secret wood they knew.

"Those children are running wild" Banna said on one of her visits. Mollie ignored such criticism. There wasn't anything she could do about it, anyway. She was far too busy and tired to try. Ned worked far too hard, he seemed almost too exhausted to think of anything else but work these days. Money became even scarcer. He spent many nights in London, staying at the cheapest hotel he could find - a Turkish bath, he explained with amusement, from which he could emerge early each morning very clean after a good night's sleep.

Mollie began to suspect he might be beginning to find the company of his secretary Betty Bliss somewhat of a consolation in London. She couldn't blame him. She was unexpectedly pregnant again and always tired, what with the children to look after, and the house to run. In a way she was quite grateful, she didn't for one moment think of Betty as some kind of threat. Ned needed some kind of compensation from the grind of his never ending workload, and she found it difficult just then to provide. Ned was not the only one to feel constantly weary.

Premature seven month twins were born at the end of May. The doctor didn't expect them to live. Such tiny little baby girls.

"They need warmth," said the village nurse firmly. She was a most remarkable woman, Mollie had come to realise. Over the years she provided help whenever there was illness in the family. Far more accessible than most local doctors, she seemed to look after the health needs of the entire village.

"Put those babies in the airing cupboard. The heat from the hot water tank is the best thing to keep them going for the next few weeks," she advised. When Mollie's mother arrived post-haste at the news of the birth, Mollie didn't know if she were glad or sorry, but at least it was another pair of hands to help while she recovered her strength. The twins needed so much coaxing to make them feed at all, especially the second one. Mollie was afraid she might not be able to produce enough milk for the two of them. Nurse Frost seemed always on hand with good advice. Mollie realised the twins would never have survived had it not been for that nurse.

"Did you know?" Mollie's mother said, "I had twins who miscarried, but they couldn't be saved." Mollie thought she could have done without that information just then. She was glad when her mother left a few weeks later.

Mollie's twins survived. They were christened, after much argument, Sylvia May and Anthea June. They flourished. In fact they won a baby magazine award for the best twins of the year. The prize money was useful for baby clothes.

Mollie found help where she could. They had a friend - perhaps Mollie conceded to herself sometimes - perhaps he was a kind of admirer of hers. He was a lonely man, who had married a cousin of his, and their only child had been born mentally retarded.

"It never does for cousins to marry, too much inbreeding," said Ned. Now Mollie's friend, with his wife dead and his son in an institution, was a lonely man. He loved children, and nothing gave him greater pleasure than to take the twins for a walk in their large double baby carriage. This allowed Mollie to rest most afternoons.

"Who cares!" Ned said. "If gossip says that perhaps he is their father, and not me. Since you and I know it isn't true people can gossip as much as they want." Ned was right, as usual, the talk soon ceased. Poor man, thought Mollie, thinking of their friend. Why shouldn't he enjoy the company of her children? It would make up for children of his own he had never been able to play with. He showed Harold and Mary his geological collection, stones he had found from all round the world. He showed them his sketch books, quite good they were too. He was such a kind, mild man. Poor Charles, he died a few years later.

"I'm glad" Ned had said, "that he was able to enjoy the company of the children for a while. He was good for them, set them off collecting stones and things. And do you remember the art club they started with Mrs Nissen, the flower painter friend of ours? That was because of Charles. They asked her to be their 'patron' - very grand sounding. She was very good to them too - had them round - gave them drawings and paintings to do."

"You notice a lot more about the shape of trees and branches and the colours of flowers if you try and paint them," Mary said. "I think I'd like to be an artist, like Baba's brother Uncle William."

Chapter 26
Country Pursuits

"I found this photograph of Charles Kynaston. Do you remember him?" Mollie asked Ned when she was next at the hospital. "Poor man, he died not long after that was taken."

"One of your fancy men," Ned smiled. "Yes, of course I remember, he was a very nice man. Very attached to you of course."

"He was rather, wasn't he?" Mollie answered skittishly, with a slight toss of the head. She had been fond of Charles, she didn't deny it. They had enjoyed each other's company. He was a well-read man, they had had a lot in common. They had even kissed sometimes when they were alone together, had sometimes been on the brink of something more.

"It was the children he was really fond of, especially the twins. He loved small children. But he was no more my fancy man, as you call it, than your secretary Betty Bliss was your fancy woman."

"I always thought you were a little jealous of Betty," said Ned.

"I couldn't have managed the business without her, you know, she was a very good secretary. She stuck by me through all those difficult years. She was very good to me you know." They both retreated into their own private thoughts for a while.

"And what about that other fancy man of yours, Cyril what's his name?" Ned asked presently. "We never did find out what became of him in the end, did we?"

"He went to Turkey didn't he, something to do with the intelligence services. He could speak Turkish you know. He disappeared mysteriously sometime in 1940, at the beginning of the second war."

"He was a wonderful piano player, and he had a very good voice. You got out your clarinet to play with us, even though you were so out of practice."

"Well, I never could play much after I got wounded, not enough puff you see."

"It was quite a trio though, wasn't it - me on the piano - you on the clarinet, Cyril singing away in that powerful voice of his." Mollie could see, although he seemed quite cheerful, that Ned was tired already. They had been talking quite long enough.

"I'll bring some more photographs tomorrow" she promised. She went home.

★

When she got home Mollie put on the radio for company. There was a nostalgic programme about Ivor Novello. It reminded her again of Cyril Hawkin. He liked those songs. Such a flamboyant man. Everything he did seemed on a larger than life scale. He arrived one day while she was organising one of her annual charity fetes in the garden, in aid of the local hospital. It must have been a few years after the twins were born. She wanted some of the things she had been given for the fete to be auctioned.

He appeared. No one could miss such an arrival. All heads turned in his direction, all conversation ceased except to speculate on who this newcomer might be. He immediately volunteered to take over the role of auctioneer. With his loud voice, his exaggerated manner, his persuasive talents, he had everything on the stall sold within minutes at unbelievably high prices. When the children presented the proceeds of the event to the local hospital it was a much higher amount than she ever managed to collect in previous years.

During the next few weeks Mollie, Ned and the exuberant Cyril, had become good friends, playing their music together, discussing politics. They both felt they had known Cyril for years.

One day, a few weeks later, while she was alone in the house, he came to say goodbye.

"I come to stay near here each summer when I'm on leave," he explained. "I hope to see you next year about this time. I shall expect you to have an even more varied selection of things for me to auction at your next fete." He kissed her, just a friendly salute, full of affection. Mollie was taken aback, but pleased all the same. It had not occurred to her that she might still seem attractive to anyone, let alone anyone as flamboyant and talented as he was. Those fetes had been a good idea. The children performed little plays, made cakes or toys, for sale, and grew flowers to sell. Mollie had always been a believer in making sure her children made a contribution of some kind to the local community. She would see they made an even greater contribution next year.

Schools had been a problem when they moved back to the village. John was sent to a boarding prep school for a short while with his cousin. He too would have to get a scholarship if he was to go to a public school. But he didn't stay long, he was so obviously miserable there. Mary missed the bus home from Farnham grammar school several times, which meant she was an hour late getting home. She didn't seem all that happy either. Mollie suspected she got bullied. The kindly neighbour who had taught the younger children for a year or two had died. Something would have to be done.

"You should never worry too much," Ned said, "Something will turn up, you'll see," and of course it did.

Two spinster ladies set up a small school in nearby Fleet, which was a godsend. They could ride the two miles there on their bicycles. It was a very small school.

"All the better," Ned said, "they will get more individual attention."

"They certainly will," Mollie said, at the beginning of the first term. "They have fifteen pupils so far, and four of those are ours."

In the summer months a kind of settled routine developed. After the children left for school each morning, Mollie would make up a picnic basket and put it in the well of the large double baby pram and push the twins in it the three miles to the Fleet swimming pool, where she would meet the children for their school lunch hour. They taught each other to swim; they rowed on the big pond, played on the tennis courts. They all enjoyed the company of the two friends who ran the club - ex- servicemen who after the war had put their savings into the development of what they called their Lido.

"Those children can all swim like fish," Mr Green, one of them said. "They could probably win Olympic medals if they tried."

John went for a while to a local grammar school. He got a scholarship to a public school, Blundells at Tiverton in Devon. Harold became a boarder at Merchant Taylor's school. The family was growing up. Even the twins were no longer babies. How will it feel, Mollie thought, after all these years of struggle, when they've gone their own ways? What then?

The girls would often come home from school together along the canal bank. The Basingstoke canal had been built during the boom of the canal age to carry sand, but it had never been used commercially. You could walk by it, swim in it, slide and skate on it in winter when it froze, even explore the wide culverts which ran under it. It was spanned by various little hand operated swing bridges. If you were in a rowing boat you had to lie on your back in the bottom of it as you skimmed expertly under the narrow gap between bridge and water. You could watch shoals of different kinds of fish as they swam unconcernedly along beside your boat; or gaze fascinated as a large pike lay in wait for them. The banks were crowded with wild flowers and butterflies. It was a kind of natural paradise. It was looked after by a water bailiff, now a very old man, called Mark, who took much pride in his conservation duties.

As you rode along the bank, negotiating the gnarled tree roots, you would smell the aroma of freshly baked bread as you passed the back of the local bakery. You could ride your bike daringly between the narrow space left between two adjacent tree trunks. Of course you might fall into the water, where the weeds were thick and dangerous, but there was always someone to pull you out.

Another winter came, and as usual in the evenings they would sit round the fire, while Mollie read to them some of her favourite books - most of Walter Scott and Jane Austen - Dickens - school set books like *Silas Marner* and *Lorna Doone*. Reading was such a pleasant relaxation for everyone.

At Christmas Mollie looked for a card from Cyril. Christmas cards were important, a chance to renew contacts, but no card came. She looked round at the children all seated at the big table, making their own cards, asking for them to be sent to uncles and aunts and cousins. Surely he could have just sent a card.

Mollie loved Christmas. The more people who came to

Christmas lunch the better. The cards, the decorated Christmas tree, the presents for excited children, carol singing round the piano - she loved the lot. This year she wished Cyril had been there. Instead she had the lovesick Harold to console. Her young son had reached the age at which young men are so often jilted. She gave him a few lines to read, she thought it might make him laugh, and feel a little less sorry for himself.

> Some men love a woman's pretty face,
> Of cleverness they need no trace.
> But underneath the glamour they then find
> A woman's impenetrable mind.
>
> They think to choose an intellectual wife
> Discussing problems of our human life.
> But then what does the poor man find
> The emptiness of an impenetrable mind.
>
> He wants a wife with common sense
> To organise the house and save the pence.
> But soon she tires of this and seeks to find
> Distraction for that impenetrable mind.
>
> He feels he'd like a wife with kindly skills
> To help him through life's trials and ills.
> But with self-pity and deception she's unkind
> She'll always know with that impenetrable mind.
>
> He thinks at last he's found what he requires,
> Someone with all the attributes that he desires.
> But then she says she does not feel inclined
> And leaves him guessing at her impenetrable mind.

Besides she felt guilty, what was she doing herself, thinking of other men, why was she not satisfied with things as they were? Who knew what she really wanted?

Finances had been improving. In the spring Ned opened an

office in Fleet. He was not away so much. They had acquired electric light, a telephone, an electric iron, a gas cooker, a radio. When the radio played the national anthem, Ned would always stand to attention until it finished playing. They listened avidly to the King's Christmas message. Ned made it feel like a religious service.

They could afford now to let the children have their way and learn to ride - the military way of course. What else in a place so full of army and ex-army personnel; the riding instructor and his daughter didn't charge that much. Ned insisted on going with them, until he fell off and was quite badly bruised.

"We are too old for joining in with that kind of thing," Mollie said. "We shall have to be content with milder forms of pleasure like playing bridge, and I expect you can still enjoy your village cricket."

Mollie and Ned played auction bridge on many an evening with a variety of friends. There was never any shortage of partners. The area was awash with ex-Indian army officers, only too happy to play to relieve the tedium of their retirement. Repatriation to England they complained, seemed to them like retirement to a foreign country. The children amused themselves by making strange sandwiches for refreshments, asking anxiously how the visitors had liked egg with rice crispies, or ham with corn flakes.

It was possible to find something amusing even in the most humdrum kind of existence, Mollie thought. Those games of auction bridge often lasted into the early hours, and you could tell a lot by the way people played their cards. Husbands and wives as partners often bickered at each other to relieve the tension in their lives, she supposed. She half thought of writing a little play about them all but never got round to it.

"That was very careless of you, not counting the trumps," probably meant, "it was very careless of you to burn the toast at breakfast this morning."

"How could you expect to win a slam without having all the aces," probably meant, "you must not be so extravagant without checking we have enough money to pay the bills." Ned was one of those who gambled and won a lot or lost a lot, while others would risk very little, so never lost or gained much.

The children played cards, 'beggar-my-neighbour' or 'fish' or nap, and of course bridge. The twins always seemed to win.

"I bet they kick each other under the table to tell each other what cards they've got," the others said in desperation. But the twins were never caught out doing any such thing. Telepathy, Mollie wondered? They were twins after all.

There were the village cricket matches, where anyone who could wield a bat or bowl a ball was invited to join the team. The heroes of a match would often be the postman and one of the younger members or the owners of the village shop. The local 'gentry' came rather further down the list, though. Ned was captain, but only ever made a few runs. The cricket dance, in the open, on a warm summer's night when everyone danced with everyone else was a gentle pleasure to remember. They got up teams to play away, like the memorable visits to the Titchborne estate. Ned never tired of telling the romantic tale of the unmasked impostor who had tried to claim the title.

Mollie couldn't get Cyril out of her mind. Would he come to the fete this year, or would she never see him again? Did he really feel some kind of interest in her? How she would welcome him if he were to come back. She thought of various pieces of music she would like them to play together. There were other things too. Did he like dancing? She imagined herself in his arms, moving to the rhythm of the music. She missed dancing. Ned had never been very good at it, but Cyril would be, he was that kind of man. Perhaps he was a tennis player, and she could learn to play with him as her partner.

A cinema had been opened in the nearby town. Mollie didn't much like cinemas, but she occasionally took the children to see 'educational' films like 'The Taming of the Shrew.' Watching it, adapted as it was, made her regret it was not more like her own idea of the original Shakespeare play. The cinema spoils things, she thought. There were news reels, but they only ever seemed to report disasters - like men and women flying around the world breaking records of one kind or another, and then disappearing over the oceans, presumed drowned, getting killed one way or another. This mania for fast machines, for records, and it wasn't only the men who were involved.

In particular Mollie didn't want to watch the news reels about reported political unrest. You would think they would have more sense, those politicians. There was a feeling, just as there had been before the last war - the war to end all wars - of restlessness, impending danger, tension, something in the air. Call it what you will, an indefinable something that said beware. Fighting in Spain - France with its riots - Italy and the strutting Mussolini - Germany with that horrible little man with a moustache called Hitler - his hysterical rallies - declaring a vendetta against the Jews - it all added up to something to be wary of. Fascism they called it, there was even a fascist rally in England. She would not let herself think that history might be about to repeat itself. She would prefer to ignore such apprehensions. She discouraged cinema-going.

"I'm sure it must be bad for your eyes" she said to the children when anyone pleaded for money to see a film.

They were both glad to see Cyril again on his next summer visit. He walked in, just as he had last time, offering to auction various items at the fete. He was as exuberant and flamboyant as ever. He might just as well have never been away.

They asked him what was going on in the diplomatic world, after all he ought to know with those secret diplomatic missions of his he said so little about. Was there any danger of German expansion, would Italy try to invade other countries? What was the government doing to prevent things getting out of hand?

"Things look as though they will settle down again," he said. They were glad to believe him.

They played music together again, of course, they even danced to the music of the gramophone, and she was right, he was the kind of dancing partner one could only dream about. They shared jokes, discussed reviews of plays and concerts. Ned was as enthusiastic as she was.

Cyril stayed his usual three weeks. He came to say goodbye. "If you came away with me," he said, when they found themselves alone, "we could visit the plays and concerts rather than just discuss the reviews of them. We could go dancing together. We could play music together. All the things I guess you have wanted over the past years, and have never had the chance to do. We could have a wonderful time together, you and I, you know that."

A new kind of life, she thought, a new interest in everything, a chance to do so many things she felt she had missed out on. It wasn't anything to do with sex, Cyril was not that kind of man, he was an intellectual. Ned could have his Betty - she was the kind of girl who would look after him all right. The children, well, they would probably look after each other. They were all growing up, and would be leaving home soon anyway. But the twins - they were much too young to leave as yet. It would be fun with Cyril, she knew that. But they were pipe dreams, she realised, just dreams, not something she would ever really consider. She shook her head. She wasn't sure how serious he was in any case.

"You know I couldn't."

"It would be fun though, wouldn't it?"

He kissed her again, in a brotherly fashion.

"That's for goodbye," he said. "I don't suppose I'll be back next year."

He went away.

Chapter 27
The Pantomime Years

"I've brought you some newspaper cuttings from those pantomimes we did," Mollie said to Ned as she arrived at his bedside on her usual visit to the hospital. Ned was very sleepy, but she persisted. He occasionally gave a kind of grunt in reply to her remarks. He was listening, she knew.

"Wake up, Ned," she pleaded once or twice but to no avail. It was difficult talking to oneself. Mary came bustling in unexpectedly.

"Sorry not to have given you more notice, but we only decided this morning that I could get away. I had some of my lectures cancelled. I thought it too good a chance to miss. I've spoken to the nurse, so I know how things are."

She gave her father a perfunctory kiss.

"It's nice to see you," he said. "Sorry I seem to be so sleepy, it's those wretched pills they keep giving me."

"We've been talking about the pantomimes," Mollie explained. "Now I'm tidying up a bit at home, I keep coming across things like these newspaper cuttings." She held out the little bundle of cuttings for her to look at.

"This one is about 'The Babes in the Wood', that's the first one you wrote, isn't it? The twins were the babes, I remember that, they were only two, and they brought the house down by unexpectedly appearing on the stage trailing your coat. I remember how unnecessarily embarrassed I felt at the time," Mary said.

"Well, I couldn't leave them at home, could I?"

"That was the one when Harold was the wicked uncle and was supposed to suggest ways of getting rid of the babes. 'Poisoned by bath or drowned in partridge' he said by mistake and I had a fit of the giggles."

"We made a lot of money for the hospital that time," Ned said. He had always acted as treasurer.

"So we should, we spent enough time making all those costumes."

"Not to mention all the time I spent collecting the props," Ned said.

"Everyone loved those pantomimes, everyone wanted to be in them."

"Half the village was."

"All those friends of Harold's from school too, when they came to stay. One of them made a splendid hind legs of a horse I remember, until the front half parted from him. That was in 'Robin Hood'."

"Do you remember Freddie the deaf boy? He repeated 'Wait and see' in that gruff voice of his every time someone pinched him to give him his cue. He loved playing the part of prime minister in 'Dick Whittington'."

"Look at this paragraph, it says 'Mrs Davis and her team do it again.' That was 'Rumpelstiltskin'."

"Nancy's knickers fell off, I remember. She didn't turn a hair - just went on dancing regardless. It's always the 'accidents' which seemed to be the funniest things and get the most laughs," Ned chuckled.

"Those were the days," said Mary. "We had a lot of fun. But we mustn't tire you too much." She couldn't help noticing how drawn he looked.

"Ned was much more lively after you came," Mollie said as they were on the way back to Strangers Corner. "I think he just gets bored with me at times."

"I think he just gets tired rather quickly," Mary replied, adding that she couldn't stay long.

"It's such a long journey all the way from Liverpool, and we always seem to be so busy. I shall have to make up for those cancelled lectures when I get back."

★

The children were always busy, especially Mary. They always had been, inventing things to do, trying out this and that. Neighbours continually complained.

"That child, climbing up into them trees, and climbing out of all them windows, it's enough to frighten my poor old mother to death."

"We only wanted to be sure," the children said, "that if there was a fire we would be able to escape from any of the upstairs rooms."

"That child shouldn't be allowed to swim so far across Fleet pond, everyone is afraid she'll drown."

"I wouldn't let that child walk on the ice on the canal like that if I were you, far too dangerous." Mollie had ignored them all, the children were quite capable of looking after themselves, she thought.

She got the idea for the pantomimes from watching the children improvise their own puppet show - making up their own fairy stories as they went along, dangling various dolls on strings above the top of an old box. Mollie would put on a Christmas pantomime in the Village Hall instead of organising the usual summer fete. She got busy writing the script straightaway - 'The Babes in the Wood' - abandoned children - she felt it a suitable subject - one she could sympathise with.

The next few years she called the Pantomime years, four in all as year followed year. It was partly a way of keeping the family together as the children were growing up. They were always there over the Christmas holiday. The boys would be home from boarding school, sometimes bringing friends with them. The girls were on hand to help with such things as making the costumes. They got quite good at using her old sewing machine. She could give her own children the main parts and coach them at home. She wanted to be busy, not to think too much about Cyril. Immersed in a make-believe world, she could sometimes pretend the real one didn't exist, that her children were not growing up, that Cyril would soon be back, that it was possible to live in a world without wars. Time could stand still.

The children started taking religion seriously. It always happens sooner or later, she thought. Hadn't she herself spent hours discussing it with Sister Veronica all those years ago at the convent. It was the local vicar who got her children interested. He was a man who, dominated by his overpowering wife, felt quite lost when she suddenly died of a heart attack. Molly felt sorry for him, inviting him to some of their boat picnics on Fleet pond. It was an expanse of water dotted with little tree-covered islands, on which they could land a boat. Herons occupied several of them, but there were others, where you could play on a sunny afternoon - climb trees - go for a short swim in the muddy water - pretend the rest of the world didn't exist. The vicar, poor man, obviously enjoyed himself. It turned out that he was quite fun to be with, chasing the children up and down trees, playing hide-and-seek, or showing them how to construct a shelter for themselves when it rained.

Of course, being a vicar, he wished the children to take church seriously, and it wasn't long before they were asking to be confirmed. Mollie was glad, she was in favour of some rite of passage as they grew up, and she had been convinced since her convent days that a Christian way of life was the ideal to aim for, even if she herself seldom went near a church. The boys were confirmed at school, the girls in the village church. The girls did take themselves rather too seriously she thought, but then girls do.

The vicar himself took Christian principles very seriously indeed. Since his wife died he had a housekeeper from the village to look after him. She became pregnant, and he offered to marry her. Mollie didn't think for a moment the child was his, he didn't seem to be that kind of a man, and she was not the most prepossessing or intelligent of girls. No, his reason must be that he felt it his Christian duty to look after her and the child the best way he knew how. There was no one else who would. Mollie rather admired him for it. Of course there was gossip, and eventually he had to move away.

She decided to accept an invitation to take the family to the sports day at Merchant Taylors school, as Harold had said he might have a chance of winning a race that year. Besides the occasion was to be graced by the presence of the Duke of York, his wife and two small daughters. The Duke stuttered, poor man, and so did Mr Leeson the headmaster.

"It g-g-g gives me g-g-g-g great p-p-p-p pleasure, to w-w-w-welcome your r-r-r-royal -h-h-h-h highness to this sss-s-s-school."

"It g-g-g-g gives me g-g-g-g-g great p-p-p-pleasure," came the answer, and speeches continued in this way for some time. Mollie thought the stutter added dignity to the occasion, made it more memorable in a strange way. Mary won an unlikely silver teapot in the sister's race. She wasn't a fast runner, nor a graceful one either. She usually looked as if she might be about to fall flat on her face. It had been an interesting occasion, one way and another.

There were more perturbing news bulletins which Mollie tried to forget. You couldn't ignore all the facts - for instance, that the strutting Italian Mussolini had invaded Abyssinia, and that although no one approved, neither was anyone prepared to stop him. You couldn't ignore the fact that the horrid little man Hitler had decided to occupy the Saar contrary to the Treaty of Versailles. She tried to ignore the rumours of German mistreatment of all those poor frightened Jews. There was the Spanish civil war, fascists against communists, each as bad as the other she imagined. There had been riots in Paris, a fascist rally in Britain. She hoped the politicians would keep England well away from all that unrest. It was much more rewarding to concentrate on the the Jubilee year of their own King George V.

"There can't have been many monarchs who have behaved as conscientiously as he has done," Ned said with pride. "We are very lucky in this country to have a king like him."

There was a Jubilee procession through the village. Ned and Mollie as proud parents watched six of their children as they paraded on horseback disguised as the six Tudor monarchs: Henry V11 (John), Henry V111 (Nancy), Bloody Mary (Mary), Elizabeth 1 (Ruth), Edward V1 (Sylvia), Lady Jane Grey (Anthea). There was a village tea party, mugs decorated with coronets were given out in the traditional way. English people congratulated themselves on the stability of their own country.

The King died early the next year.

"End of an era," Ned said. No one realised at the time how true that would prove to be. There was tension in the air, people were restless, you could feel it everywhere - so many changes.

Banna bought a bungalow which was down the lane near the Haven.

"I don't want to stay in London any longer," she confided. "Besides, I miss you and the children, I need to see more of you while I still can." The children didn't care much for this arrangement.

"She's always picking on us, always telling us what we should be doing," Ruth said. Mollie wished Banna would stop being so critical. There were moments of light relief, as when Ruth threw a lump of sugar at her and hit her on the nose. To everyone's surprise, Banna burst out laughing. But it was an uncomfortable arrangement to have her so near none the less.

The children were leaving home. They thought Harold might get a scholarship to university but he didn't. Banna offered to pay for a place for him, but he refused.

"Why should she pay for me," he said. "If I'm not clever enough to get a scholarship, there is probably no point in my going there anyway." Ned agreed. Instead he got a job in an office in London, which he hated, found himself a small flat, discovered London low life was exciting and stimulating in contrast, and brought a succession of girls home at weekends to introduce them to the family. Mary too left school. She got a job nursing at a local hospital. Nancy, who from now on wanted to be called Anne, left school and joined the Red Cross working at a school for handicapped children. John was still away at boarding school. The house had suddenly gone quiet, too quiet.

One of Harold's friends who was up at Oxford arrived one day and said he had come to say goodbye.

"I have a pistol you see, and some friends and I are going to fight in the Spanish civil war against the fascists. Someone has got to stop them," he said.

As if, thought Mollie, a few young lads with pistols could stem the rising tide. She heard later he had got turned back from entering Spain, the border had been closed.

"You have to admire his spirit though," said Ned.

Edward V111 had become King, in succession to his father.

"The politicians are afraid of what that spoilt brat may do," Ned said. "He's nothing like his conscientious father. He has far too much charm to be good for him. He is self opinionated, without really understanding what he is talking about." If Ned could say something like that about royalty something must really be seriously wrong.

Ned decided he would like to become a Liberal politician, he had always been a member of the Liberal party. He spoke at meetings and at the hustings in Hyde Park. He had some original ideas, and strong views about how to avert a war, ideas not often shared with other members of the party. Besides he lacked a politician's ready wit in sidestepping awkward questions.

"His heart is in the right place," one of his Masonic friends was heard to say, "but he is much too nice to play the politicians' game. Pity though."

There were more and more rumours about the King and his attachment to a divorced American woman whose great ambition, it was said, was to become Queen of England.

"I think," Ned said, when the King was forced by the prime minister to either abandon her or abdicate, "that Stanley Baldwin has handled a difficult situation very well. We are well rid of him and his American woman, and his unhealthy sympathy for German politicians."

His younger brother, the Duke of York, George V1 as he then became, had wept, it was said, at the terrible prospect of having to become King. He was crowned next year. The ex-king departed to France and married his lady love.

Another crisis, a family one. A letter had come from the housekeeper saying that Aunt Penelope had become seriously deranged, and could no longer be left without strict supervision.

'She is quite violent at times, and needs professional care,' the letter said. Banna departed the next day. She left an empty house behind her, saying she must go and look after her.

Various gloomy items of news were discussed - Americans over -farming their land and creating a huge dust bowl causing the ruin of all the farmers there - Americans always did seem to do things on too grand a scale; Germany reclaiming more land; dreadful rumours about the maltreatment of Jews in Germany. It was not so easy now to ignore what was going on, all those poor frightened Jews trying desperately to get resettled in Palestine.

"There is going to be a war, you know," said the wife of one of the Indian colonels they knew, as they settled down to play bridge one evening. It was the first time Mollie had been forced to really face such a possibility.

"Oh, no," said Mollie, "I still don't believe it. No one would be so foolish as to contemplate such a thing, not even the Germans, especially the Germans, after the terrible experiences of the last war."

The papers were full of bad news. The Hindenberg airship blew up killing most of its passengers; there was Russia and Stalin and his mock trials and executions; there was the Japan-China war, and more ominously a German-Japanese pact.

It was decided the family should move into Greengates, the empty house vacated by Banna. It was small but rent-free. The school in Fleet had closed, Ruth and the twins went to another one in a small local town. Mary went to London to a teaching hospital to train as a nurse.

Neville Chamberlain said on the radio that it was 'Peace in our time.' Banna was very insistent that Mollie and the three youngest children should come to a holiday camp in Blackpool.

"You all need a holiday. Besides you never know," she said, "this may be the last opportunity I shall ever have to see you and the children again if there is to be another war."

If there was to be another war it wasn't likely to be declared just yet, Mollie thought. So they went. The children seemed to enjoy themselves, winning all kinds of swimming prizes.

Poland was invaded, Germany challenged to withdraw.

'I have to tell you now, no such undertaking has been given, and in consequence we are now at war with Germany,' said the Prime Minister's voice over the wireless.

Chapter 28
Chaos

Mollie and the three children, Ruth, Sylvia and Anthea, managed after considerable delays to get a taxi to Blackpool station. After a long wait they were at last allowed on board a train going south. Mind you, like many others, they had to stand in the corridor surrounded by their own and other people's luggage over which people clambered at intervals with subdued irritation. The train was crowded with young men in uniform, carrying army kit bags over their shoulders, and then dumping them down inadvertently onto people's feet. They talked loudly. and constantly as they moved up and down the train. Harassed looking army officers passed by, looking anxious as they peered into the dark crowded interiors of compartments.

When the train stopped at a large city station, crowds of bewildered children carrying gas masks in cardboard boxes over their shoulders stood patiently waiting. On their coats they sported buff-coloured labels, on which were written in large letters names and addresses and destinations.They were shepherded by official looking women into carriages marked 'children only'. They tearfully waved goodbye to the anxious looking adults left stranded on the receding platform. And then they were shepherded off the train again at some small wayside station or other, looking even more bewildered. The train proceeded very slowly. Everything became very dark as daylight faded - the 'blackout' allowed only the dimmest pinpoint of light to be seen anywhere. Everyone was hungry and thirsty and very tired.

"It's like a train carrying people to hell," Sylvia said dramatically.

They got to London at last, air raid sirens wailing round them, and even got a taxi - eventually - across London to Waterloo to catch a train to Fleet. As the train pulled out there were more soldiers, more bewildered children, more porters anxiously shouting information at each other.

Mollie didn't know what time it was - her watch had stopped. They were eventually deposited at Fleet station. Some kindly soldiers helped them off with their luggage. It was very dark, and there seemed to be no one about. How was she to get home to their house three miles away, with three children and all that luggage? Ned she knew was in London. There seemed nothing for it but to try and walk there. She gave one case to the twins to carry between them, a smaller one to Ruth, and tried to move the biggest one herself. It was no use, she could only carry it about a hundred yards before she had to put it down again. At this rate it would take them all night to get home. Perhaps, she thought, we could stop and ask a kind householder we know to help us, despite the lateness of the hour. Then she realised it would be some way to walk even to the nearest house, let alone to one where she had friends.

A car appeared out of the darkness, the driver someone she didn't recognise. He must also have got off the train she supposed, although she hadn't noticed him on the platform. He pulled up beside them.

"Where to?" he asked, as he opened the car doors and helped them and their luggage aboard. He drove them slowly home, his lights dim, feeling his way in the dark. He unloaded the luggage and carried it in for them. Just as she was about to thank him for his help he seemed to disappear. She never did discover who that kind Samaritan had been. She made some tea and they went to bed. Never had Mollie felt so weary.

Why, she kept asking herself, why was I so foolish as to listen to Banna's demand that we go and see her in Blackpool? It was against my better judgment to go for such a holiday in such uncertain times, I should not have been so easily persuaded, she sharply told herself. I shouldn't have been made to feel guilty if I'd refused.

War again, with Germany, only with more lethal weapons to hand than in the last war. I have to believe it now, she thought, as she unpacked next morning. Would they have to face a new war - long days and nights waiting to hear about inevitable causalities -

the fear of defeat and invasion - the possibility of starvation? She learnt in the last war what submarines could do to interrupt supplies. What she dreaded most was the thought of all the bombs that might be dropped on them. There would be no way to stop it this time. All you could do was hold your breath and carry on. How could this be happening again after all that talk of peace, and the League of Nations. Will good intentions always be the road to hell?

Harold had been called up, with many of his friends. Mary was in London where the first bombs were likely to be dropped. Ned said he would volunteer to rejoin the army. Her sister-in-law Connie and her son Francis sailed off to Canada as evacuees, her brother Arthur got married to a Scottish girl, and soon after decided to get divorced.

Ned was sent off to organise a nearby camp, a lengthy bike ride away. Girls they knew joined the forces in the WAAFS or ATS or WRNS - such a bewildering array of letters, Mollie thought. Some decided to be VADs or NAs. Older women joined the WVS. Some became land army girls.

Ned said someone suggested they buy a piglet and fatten it on household scraps to help feed the family in what were likely to be such difficult days ahead. "We'll make sure we provide for ourselves as best we can," he explained. The pig was called Henry.

First-aid classes were given for civilians. At Crookham one of the ex-Indian army doctors was commandeered.

"I can't quite see," said Mollie, "what use information on snake bites and obscure Indian diseases will be to us here." But everyone listened politely. She was made a Red Cross commandant, with a team of drilled volunteers available should they be needed. Everyone started to practise bandaging and treating people for shock, and were shown how to deal with broken limbs. The twins made excellent volunteer patients to practise on.

Air raid shelters became a familiar sight in many houses or gardens. Should you walk along the canal banks you soon realised they were discreetly dotted with concrete machine gun posts, while great anti-tank concrete bollards poked their heads out of the water. It was surprising how well organised things were in what seemed no time at all. Blackout curtains were put up everywhere, air raid wardens on bicycles paraded the streets at night checking for infringements. Gas masks had been issued and hilarity broke out as people practised how to use them in every kind of situation.

"Picture us trying to tell a poor patient what to do through one of those things," Mary reported, "when we practised on the wards the patients were half frightened to death at first, and they couldn't understand a word we said. They ended up laughing at all the rude noises we produced."

Identity cards were issued. Metal identity bracelets were worn, ready to identify you should you get killed. Worn day and night and everywhere, they were not to be removed until the war ended. Ration books were issued. Mollie got used to the idea that anyone arriving for an overnight stay came to the house equipped with two jars, one containing the week's sugar, and the other a week's butter ration.

'Aliens', those of other nationalities who might be considered a threat to England, were sent out of the way to 'safe camps' for the duration. Mollie thought sometimes it was as much for the protection of the aliens themselves, as for the protection of the populace against would-be spies. Everyone began to suspect the loyalty of the ex-king, the Duke of Windsor. He was banished to some distant island as governor.

Mollie's lady help reported a conversation she overheard between the twins.

"Those twins are a caution," she said, "do you know what I heard them talking about the other day? Children have the strangest ideas. Me and mother had a good laugh over it."

"What was that, then?" Mollie asked.

"They think there is a spy living in the house opposite. They said mysterious people come and visit there, usually after dark, and there are strange noises going on sometimes."

"I wish you'd told me this before. What else did they say?" Mollie was horrified.

"They didn't mean no harm by it. They said as they saw a light flickering in that garden the other night, a signal like to some enemy spy."

"Don't repeat that to anyone on any account, will you, that's how stupid rumours start," Mollie said.

She accosted the twins with the information given her, but it turned out they had already written a note to the neighbour accusing her of being a spy.

"We thought if we put a note through her letter box, she would know we knew what she was doing, and then she would have to stop."

Mollie was really angry, and sent them to apologise and retrieve the note.

"She has visitors at night," she explained, "because she's a musician, and plays the violin very well. People have been visiting her to arrange for her to play in a concert to entertain the troops. I expect the flickering light you saw was her torch as she saw her visitors to the gate. I hope you are both thoroughly ashamed of yourselves."

Australian, New Zealand and Canadian uniforms appeared in the village pubs, the whole area was awash with soldiers from around the world. Barrage balloons floated defiantly, like bloated sliver fish in the sky above. People could be heard humming the tunes of derogatory songs like 'Run Rabbit Run' or 'We'll hang out the washing on the Siegfried Line." Air raid wardens showed people how to put out firebombs with something called a stirrup pump. Then everyone waited, and waited, not knowing but dreading what might come next.

Germany invaded Norway and Denmark, Holland, Belgium, and then France. Old men and young boys joined the Home Guard, to imagine in their dreams of capturing shot down German pilots single -handed, or repelling an invasion with whatever inadequate or ancient weapons they might have to hand. Churchill became prime minister.

The Dunkirk catastrophe erupted - the retreat from France, with all those gallant little boats sailing out to bring many of the retreating soldiers safely home.

"Do you remember Mons and the Angel of Mons in the last war?" Ned said. "It felt then as though, even in retreat, God was on our side. It's just the same now. Some divine providence seems to have brought down that great fog to protect as many of the men as possible as they struggled home across the English Channel. It seems like some kind of proof that God is on our side, that eventually we will win."

"If the Germans get here they will think," John said, as the word Crookham was obliterated from the Crookham St. Cash Stores shop front, "that they've landed in Cornwall, at a place called St. Cash."

"I don't know about the Germans, but it's getting impossible for Englishmen to find their way around with all those signposts gone," said his father.

A next door neighbour came to see Mollie.

"The children have been practising a favourite game of theirs, of swooping down unexpectedly on passing soldiers from that tree in my back garden. I thought perhaps I should tell you. I don't see there is any harm in it myself." They went to watch, making sure not to be seen.

"If they were Germans we could probably kill some of them," Sylvia said.

"My turn," said Anthea, grabbing the rope that hung from the tree as two soldiers could be seen approaching along the road. She and Anthea and their two friends were perched high in the branches overhead.

"Wah wah wah wah wahhhhhh..." Anthea shouted, in as blood-curdling a way as she could manage, and swung down on the rope at the two passing men. The soldiers laughed and gave her a friendly wave as she swung back again into the branches.

"You always get the nice ones," her friend complained. "Now it's my turn" as four more soldiers strolled by.

"You didn't mind my telling you, I hope," said Mollie's friend. Mollie just laughed.

The real war started - the almost constant sound of wailing sirens, the pop pop pop of anti-aircraft fire and the nightly display of searchlight beams across the sky, like some weird kind of aerial ballet. People got used to the drone of the German bombers as they homed in on London and other big cities. Sometimes the whole of London seemed to be going up in flames. There was the whine of the engines of fighter planes overhead, as dare-devil young pilots chased off the invading German planes as best they could. Everyone watched the news reels now. They showed the devastation caused by the bombs in London and other large cities. All those air raid casualties, those terrible city scenes that numbed the imagination. People digging for survivors along demolished streets,
with perhaps a single upstairs floor left gaping, a bed on it suspended in midair.

"So macabre," Ned said.

"How terrible for someone to go out to post a letter, like that friend of John's, and come back a short while after to find they have no house, no family left, just a pile of rubble to mark where they were buried by the blast."

In London people took to the underground stations as a nightly shelter. It was like spending the night in a miniature underground village, she thought, on a rare trip to London to visit Mary in hospital one day. Each family had its own allotted space, there were hot drinks to be had, even a kind of improvised street entertainment to be enjoyed as hundreds huddled together there for mutual comfort. Mollie was glad to get back to Crookham.

When the phone rang a few days later it was Mary's voice she heard.

"I thought I'd better ring to tell you I'm all right, in case they mention on the news that the hospital has been hit. Not many casualties, thank goodness. I was in casualty and within a few minutes the department was awash with water from the shattered water pipes.We had to rescue floating equipment besides trying to help the injured."

Civilian casualties mounted as raids intensified. The palace was bombed, and the King and Queen spent many hours visiting the stricken areas to give what comfort they could. Churchill made heroic speeches. Heroic firemen fought the flames as night after night half London seemed to be on fire. Heroic wardens dug people out of the mounting piles of rubble.

The comic radio programme ITMA was broadcast, providing much needed light relief.

Strange, Mollie thought, how certain phrases stick in your mind, become part of an everyday system of communications. 'Can I do you now sir?' or 'it's being so cheerful as keeps me going', were bequeathed to posterity through the glum character of Mona Lot.

"This is Funf speaking," said a voice behind her as she stood in the kitchen - Funf was the ITMA archetypal evil German. Mollie was startled, someone must have been reading her thoughts. She laughed when she saw who it was standing there.

"I've come to say goodbye" said Cyril Hawkin. "I'm being sent off on some rather uncertain foreign mission somewhere."

She knew from his tone of voice that he thought he was unlikely to come back.

"No use thinking of the might-have-beens," he continued cheerfully. He kissed her, an affectionate farewell kiss.

"You won't forget me will you?" he said lightly.

"Of course not."

"Tell Ned I'm sorry I missed him." He was gone, walking briskly out of the house, out of their lives. Mollie sat and played the piano for quite some while.

The open camp fields where once they all collected blackberries together, were now occupied by a vast army camp. Soldiers appeared in assorted uniforms - free French, Norwegian, Belgian, Danish - Polish even. More ships were sunk, and countless sailors drowned. Japan bombed the US Fleet at Pearl Harbour, Japan and America declared war, and shortly afterwards America declared war on Germany.

"At least we're not fighting alone anymore," Ned said. "Things should improve from now on."

The Women's Institute provided much appreciated comic relief for everyone in the village. They organised 'village hops' for the soldiers in the village hall, where everyone joined in the dancing and sang songs like, 'There'll be bluebirds over, the white cliffs of Dover' and 'a nightingale sang in Berkeley Square.'

Villagers were entertained with Mollie's war-time sketches - how to get entangled with a stirrup pump; how to truss up patients with strange bandaging techniques; how to provide even more outlandish cookery recipes than those now provided by the government; how to make good use of the discarded contents of your dustbin, were enthusiastically acted out. There was never a lack of subjects on which to base some kind of hilarious skit.

Harold got married to an Australian girl called Sheila, who could sing and swim rather well.

Mary came sometimes on a visit from London.

"Clapham Junction was bombed last night, sorry I'm later than I said I'd be. I walked the seven miles across Tweezledown from Aldershot. The rail line to Fleet was blocked. I had to ask the engine driver himself where we were going, no one else seemed to know."

"You must be hungry," Mollie said.

"Oh, not too bad," Mary answered cheerfully, "you know how it is, we shared things in the carriage between us. I had some chocolate, and someone else a sandwich or two, and someone else had a whole packet of biscuits. We even got a swig of water each."

"It must have been very dark, up there on Tweezledown?"

"I did lose my way once, but there were a couple of Canadian soldiers coming home late to their camp, and they put me right. There is usually somebody or other about up there to help if need be."

Next night her mother woke her in the early hours.

"Is that bombs I can hear?" she asked anxiously. Mary listened, and counted.

"Yes, but they are not very near. Probably some lone German pilot off-loading. Someone will let you know if they need your help." She went to sleep again. It was only then Mollie realised how familiar an experience the sounds of falling bombs must have become to her.

Germany invaded Russia. There was admiration for the heroic convoys being sent to help the Russians. It was difficult to shut out the picture in your mind at night as you went to sleep thinking of those freezing drowning men in the wastes of the arctic seas. Singapore fell to the Japanese, who took a great number of prisoners of war.

Harold was posted abroad, she thought to Burma, though of course neither of them mentioned it - (careless talk costs lives). It was said that if the Japanese didn't kill you, you would probably die of some strange jungle fever. She said goodbye to her handsome son knowing that even if he did come back, he would be a changed man. War did that to fighting men.

John wanted to join up.

"You'll be much more use to everyone if you get your medical qualification first. Besides, being in London is like being in the front line anyway, you'll need all your skills for treating London bomb casualties," his father said.

Mary joined the QAs. - that is Queen Alexandra's Imperial Military Nursing Service - reserve. She was shipped off to somewhere or other in the Middle East.

Ned became ill and was invalided out of the army again. After all these years that piece of shrapnel in his shoulder had shifted, and found its way at last near to the surface of his chest. An operation was needed to finally remove it. For a while he needed looking after.

Older people in the village sometimes needed help.

"I want you to go and clean Miss Frost's house for her," Mollie bade the twins one day.

"Must we?" grumbled Sylvia. "We were going to play in our tree house today."

"She's not well, poor woman. She can't look after herself properly anymore, and she needs your help." Sylvia wrinkled up her nose. She had heard talk about how dirty that house had become.

"Do we have to? Can't someone else do it?"

"Well, considering that you wouldn't be here at all if it were not for her - she saved your lives remember when you were born - I think you should, don't you?"

Ruth joined the WRNS and went to Portsmouth in a smart naval uniform.

Harold's daughter Joanna was born, and Mollie loved having Sheila and the baby living close by.

The twins were machine-gunned in their upstairs classroom while at school one day. Quick-witted teachers had the children on the floor just in time to avoid injuries.

"The plane was so close we could see the pilot as he flew low past the windows. He looked at us with a glint in his eyes," Anthea reported indignantly, "he meant to kill us, I know he did. He could see we had school uniforms, but he was out to get us just the same."

Sylvia became ill - with diphtheria the doctor said, and he arranged for her to go to the nearest fever hospital.

"We must prevent an epidemic at all costs," he said.

"She's staying at home," said Mollie firmly.

When the ambulance arrived Mollie sent it packing. She just stood in front of the house and refused the men entry.

"I don't believe she has diphtheria, and if she has being sent to hospital will certainly kill her. Do you know what her temperature is? You can't move her now." The men went. Sylvia came out in a scarlet fever rash.

"You were right," said John. "If they had put her in a diphtheria ward she would certainly have died. Mothers often know better than doctors, I told the specialist that one day on his rounds. The look he gave me - I'll probably be told I've failed all the exam papers he set us."

Chapter 29
The Beginning Of The End

Mollie had been so lost in thinking in her rambling way of the events of the Second World War, that she felt quite bemused when Ruth came to take her to see Ned at the hospital next day. The war - the Second World War - in a strange way, had suddenly seemed to become more real than the present day. She felt she had been on a long journey, so many thoughts packed into one night's restless sleep. She decided to take some letters she had kept to show Ned. He had been interested in those photographs she had taken to show him yesterday after all, so perhaps he would like to talk about the letters.

"Look," she said hopefully, as she sat down by his bed, "I've brought some wartime letters I kept, I thought you might be interested." Ned only grunted sleepily.

"He's very tired," the nurse said.

"We certainly produced some independent children between us, didn't we?" she said, "These letters from the children seem quite interesting."

Ned grunted again. She realised it was hard for him to focus on what she was saying.

"I'll read you the interesting bits" insisted Mollie, perching her glasses on her nose. Not that she thought he would be listening much, but it was something to do while she sat there.

"This one is from Mary, when she was posted to the Middle East, remember?" Ned had always been interested in travel. "She always did write interesting letters, but what awful writing she had even then, I can hardly make it out. Let me see."

"She talks about the journey out to her desert hospital. It must have been quite a journey - through the Mediterranean, enjoying that's what she says - enjoying a spectacular storm and watching out for U boats.

Then they crossed the desert in an open Nairn bus expecting to be attacked by brigands any minute. She mentions that dressing gown she used to wear, the one she bought in the Street called Straight - the street mentioned in the Bible. They had stopped for a few hours in Damascus. Hot, she says, it was very hot. They had to be careful about heat stroke. Very uncomfortable I should think with those sand storms."

Ned didn't say anything. Perhaps something humorous would rouse him.

"Remember that joke she told us about the matron in the hospital? 'There is a horrible regular army QA Matron in charge here. We discarded our black stockings because it's so hot - lots of nurses do in other hospitals - and she put up a notice saying 'All nurses will wear black stockings and regulation shoes at all times, and nothing else.' We didn't dare follow instructions to the letter, though we did think of it. Now we all have prickly heat."

Was she mistaken, or did she see a faint smile on Ned's face?

"Here is another dramatic bit - about when it rained in the desert for the first time in years."

"All the wards are built half underground to keep them cooler. Half an hour after the rain started the wards were flooded several feet deep. A wall collapsed, and we were running around trying to rescue patients floating off their beds."

"Here is a letter from Harold," Mollie continued, encouraged to go on.

"I'm in hospital with a bout of malaria, hence this opportunity to get this posted to you. The jungle is stifling. I find some of the officers very intolerant, so feel at times that I have to stand up for the native troops. I seem to have been here for ever. They say we are the forgotten army."

There was no response from Ned this time. Perhaps he would like to hear about Ruth.

"This is one from Ruth from her naval base. Let's see - she says they work hard and have fun, and it's easy to get on with everyone there."

There was no response at all from Ned. She prodded him, to say goodbye - still no response. He must be very fast asleep. She gathered up the letters, and quietly left the ward.

Back home she sat down on her favourite chair. She knew there was nothing more that could be done for Ned.

★

She sat dreaming, one of those dreams that even while she dreamed she knew it had some significance beyond the dream itself. She was in the dream, but watching herself as if she were outside it. She was young again, frightened, and feeling terribly alone. A man stood beside her. She recognised that it was the man she had so mysteriously encountered from time to time during her lifetime. It was the man who called himself Mr. Hutchinson, the man from her past she knew yet didn't know. They were walking together into a dark house, he was holding her hand, encouraging her.

"There is nothing to be worried about, everything is to be taken care of," he was saying, "I promise you that. I'll see you are protected in the future."

She woke abruptly, knowing the dream meant something, but she wasn't quite sure what. It was very quiet. It was dark and she was feeling cold. She shivered and wrapped her coat carefully around her again. As she did so she examined her gnarled hands as if they no longer belonged to her, as if she expected them to be other than they were. They were old hands that lay in her lap, not those of the young girl she had just been dreaming of.

Then she found herself dozing off again, retreating back into her dream. Mr. Hutchinson was still there in her mind, but it was wartime now. A few people standing stunned in the after silence of an exploded bomb, gazing at a great crater in the middle of the road, the shattered houses round about were crazily balanced at strange angles, the dust rising gently into the acrid air.

"He's dead" someone said presently, as they gazed at a man lying sprawled on the road. Mollie looked at the face. She knew it was Mr. Hutchinson. She woke again abruptly, feeling the physical discomfort of a nightmare's residue.

Again she slept. She was on the mountain-side in Wales, with the old crow and the strange woman.

'Seven is seven and one is eight' she heard the voice repeat. 'What is lost shall be found.'

It was some time later when she stumbled up to bed. She turned on her radio. She needed distraction, music would help her to settle her thoughts. As it happened the radio was playing old wartime tunes. That's what wartime did to you, left your head full of snatches of songs, sanitised news headlines, deep feelings too numbed to express. At least they were playing a cheerful tune this time. Like snatches of song, vivid war memories came flooding back.

'Oh what a beautiful morning,
Oh what a beautiful day,
I've got a wonderful feeling,
Everything's going my way.'

"That's a very cheerful song," she remembered saying to Ned, the first time she heard it played.

"That's because" Ned said, "of our victory over that German General Rommel at the desert battle of El Alamein. It's the turning of the tide, the beginning of the end, that's what people are beginning to feel now."

"But all that killing," she had protested, no one has any right to feel cheerful while people are still killing each other everywhere."

'Bouncing bombs have breached the dam walls, the German Ruhr valley arms factories have been put out of action,' was a news item she remembered. She could picture to herself those deadly metal balls skimming lightly over the water, like the stones children bounce over the surface of a pond.

"All the arms factories in the valley are supposed to have been flooded out," Ned said. Mollie thought of a wall of water engulfing those thousands of workers as they struggled and drowned.

"Now Mussolini has been deposed, and the Italians have changed sides and joined the allies instead," he continued, "the war may soon be over." She was pleased Mussolini had gone, she never could stand those pictures of that smug and haughty face.

There had been a picture in the paper of the summit meeting in

Teheran - those three old gentlemen - Roosevelt and Stalin and Churchill, sitting there together in a row on a bench - looking as if they might be discussing the weather - but instead, as the paper had explained in detail, they were plotting the future of the world.

It was a time of great restlessness. Everyone got used to seeing American soldiers about the streets. 'Over-paid, over-sexed and over here' was the word.

"They even have to be provided with cold-storage refrigerators so they can have ice cold drinks whenever they want. They are far too soft to win a battle," a neighbour had remarked scathingly, "they have no idea what real hardship is."

"They'll soon learn," Ned had said, "we can't win without them."

Tanks rolled lumbering along the roads, long columns of armoured cars passed by, jeeps bustled about everywhere, planes flew distractedly overhead. No one was supposed to say so, but the planned invasion of France was obviously about to take place. Ned had been right, the defeat of Rommel had been the beginning of the end.

It was D Day and all those hopeful young men stormed the French beaches - those who would never come back, those who would be maimed, those who would come back with their medals and tales of triumph. Amongst them her nephew Francis who had joined up and returned from Canada to take part in the invasion of France, would he come back? Rations were getting shorter. "We'll have to eat Henry the pig," Mollie suggested one day, but the twins wouldn't hear of it.

"We can't eat Henry," they said in shocked voices, "how can you ever suggest such a thing?" Henry was sold, but the twins were not told it was to the butcher.

V1 and then V2 rockets had begun to hit London, so much more destruction, so many more casualties. People were more afraid. There was something eerie and terrifying about the rockets, silent death they called it.

"Why don't the Germans surrender?" she asked Ned, "It must be obvious by now they will eventually lose the war." Mollie resented the unnecessary loss of yet more lives.

Despite setbacks the invasion proceeded. Paris fell, and the cheering crowds along the Champs Elyseé greeted de Gaulle as their liberator. Brussels was entered, there were more pictures of crowds cheering triumphant soldiers. Soviet troops still occupied Poland. The Poles were devastated.

"There is only one thing worse than a German occupation, and that is a Russian one." They vehemently complained at what they saw as their betrayal.

The American president Roosevelt died.

"He's been a sick man for some time," Ned said. "I'm afraid that may have affected the outcome of those summit negotiations. The Russians need to be watched, Stalin will be all out for whatever he can get, anyone that thinks differently is a fool." Reservations about the agreements were already being voiced. Russians stole a march on the allies and walked into Berlin.

At last the Germans did surrender, when Hitler had fled to his bunker with his lady love and then committed suicide.

"Reading about his death is like reading the script of some unlikely grand opera plot," Mollie said.

Naturally everyone went mad as they celebrated victory on V E day, cheering the royal family, dancing in the streets, euphoric goodwill that would evaporate with the morning's hangover.

"Now we can get back to normal," the neighbours said.

"It'll be a long time before anything feels normal again, if ever," Mollie warned.

Anne was asked to go and help at the notorious Belsen concentration camp, now liberated, to give out daily hopeful messages in various languages to the stricken inmates.

"She's very young," Mollie had said, "do you think she will be all right? News about what they have found in those concentration camps turns my stomach - those piles of emaciated bodies and the terrible experiences of those still living - so what it must be like to be there in person I cannot even imagine. All those stranded people of differing nationalities, trying to find their way back home, trying to find lost relatives, trying to rediscover who they really are themselves." Anne insisted she wanted to go.

The war wasn't yet quite over. There was still Japan to be defeated by the Americans. Atom bombs were dropped, the

Japanese surrendered. There were graphic reports of the terrifying effects of radiation.

"What have those Americans done, unleashing such a terrible new weapon?" Mollie said to Ned. "I can still remember talking to those students at Cambridge when I was there, and saying then that science was getting out of hand, and look where it has got us now. They should never have allowed that atom bomb to be invented."

"It shortened the war," Ned said. "Now Harold will be able to come home, if he's still alive." Stories of the terrible sufferings of the Japanese prisoners of war had been filtering through, and there had been no letters from him for quite a while. But she instinctively knew he was safe. The children had all come home safely.

Mollie sat up, she wanted to be done thinking about those war years, she wanted to forget all about them now. It had been a kind of obsession, thinking and dreaming over all that war time history in the last few days. She was but half awake, half asleep, and the memories persisted.

Chapter 20
All Change

It had been a bewildering time, settling down again after that war. It seemed like some strange game of travelling musical chairs. Some members of the forces came home on leave and went away again. Some people who were in England were called up and sent abroad to replace those who were being permanently released. Those who came home had to find jobs, those whose jobs had kept them at home were made redundant. Some who were married got divorced, while many others couldn't wait to get married.

War changed everyone. Those who had left and experienced life in foreign lands and been scarred in varying degrees by the inevitable brutality of war, were not the same care-free individuals who had left the country years ago. How could they be? Many of those who returned were met by strangers who had once been their partners, for wives and sweethearts too had changed. There were fathers whose children had grown beyond recognition, or perhaps whom they had never seen before, even perhaps children in the family who had been fathered by other men.

Some came home knowing parents, sisters, brothers, friends were no more, many having been killed in the blitz. Family homes had been demolished, even whole streets where once they lived were now just piles of rubble.

Things changed for Mollie too. Her brother Arthur was called up to replace home-coming doctors. He died on his way out to the Middle East. Mollie had always been fond of Arthur despite his moods. Her son John's medical skills, now that he was qualified, were needed in Germany. Aunt Penelope had died, the house sold. Aunt Fanny's nursing friend had died, as well as the patient they cared for between them. Aunt Ada's partner was dead. The three isolated old ladies had moved in together into a seaside bungalow in Worthing.

"You and your mother should've let me investigate your Aunt Penelope's affairs years ago," Ned said. "One of the lawyers who had been in charge of your affairs is dead, the other dying. Between them they have embezzled most of what she owned. The rest is left to charity. I'm sure she didn't understand what was going on, even before she became ill. I've often warned you not to trust those lawyers."

Ned and Mollie had moved to their present house and called it 'Strangers Corner.'

"Just the kind of house I've always wanted," Mollie said as soon as she saw it. "Unlike Greengates it'll be large enough to accommodate everyone when they start coming home. Such a pretty garden too - and so much open space for everyone."

Mary came home on leave, saying she would have to go back to Egypt in four weeks' time.

"It's very strange," she said to Mollie on her first night in the new house, "but I could have sworn there was a woman in that bedroom, and then she seemed to vanish."

"Oh, it was the local ghost I expect," her mother said unperturbed, "the villagers all talk about her. I've never seen her myself."

Perhaps, Mollie thought rather thankfully, I've lost the power I once seemed to have of experiencing all those strange phenomena. It's certainly a long time since anything like that has happened to me.

Anne came home, pregnant and married to a very handsome Polish officer with romantic Polish manners who was called Jan. She had been through the ceremony twice already, once conducted by army officials, and once by a Catholic priest.

"You'd better get married at an English registry office, now you're back in England, just to make sure its legal here," Ned said.

Rations became ever more restricted. Jan set to to make the land belonging to Strangers Corner into a market garden. He dared not ever go back to Poland, he feared for his life he said, the Russians would arrest him.

Ned became a director of several companies - a racing dog track and a soft drinks company among others. It pleased him to be driven in a chauffeur driven car to the various meetings he attended round the countryside.

"They call me a trouble-shooter," he said. "They use me to put a company back on its feet, and then ask me to take on some other struggling concern to do the same."

Harold came home, tired and bewildered, but delighted to see his wife and meet his entrancing little daughter. He and Sheila and little Joanna moved into that now unoccupied bungalow Greengates.

Mary didn't go back to Egypt. After hectic negotiations she stayed to get married to Harold's friend David.

Ruth came home, and went away again to a London hospital to obtain a nursing qualification. Sylvia went to join a family on the Danish island of Mön. Anthea went to Farnham Art School which had once been run by her Great Uncle William, the landscape painter. Harold spent his days in London, learning to be an accountant.

"I feel like Mrs Bennet in Jane Austen's novel *Pride and Prejudice* - to see all these daughters married off," Mollie said to Ned. "Mrs Bennet was right, you know, it's a mother's responsibility to see all her children get properly married. Any marriage is better than no marriage, I've always thought that. At the moment it's three down and four to go. The girls may find it difficult, there's always a shortage of men after a war."

Ruth got married to Peter, whom she had met in the Navy. Sylvia got married to another John, who knew a lot about horses. John got married to a girl who had been brought up in Canada.

"Six down, and one to go," said Mollie, with a laugh in her voice.

Anne, her husband Jan and their two little girls had emigrated to Canada by then, and Mollie arranged for Anthea to visit them.

"I'm not like your father," she said, "It's a very long time since I enjoyed travelling, but I'll come with you if you like."

To Canada they went, and Anthea married a surveyor called Ralph, a friend of Jan's.

"There," said Mollie triumphantly, "I told you they would all get married." She and Ned enjoyed their subsequent visits to the two families in Canada immensely.

"So much less crowded, such a feeling of freedom, so much less convention, so much more care people have for one another. They just enjoy themselves," she explained to her friends. "If I were young again, that's where I'd go."

"And so would I," said Ned.

"How many grandchildren is that we have, about fifteen by now I suppose," Ned said "and several more will appear no doubt over the next few years."

When her children were all settled, Mollie began to feel restless again. There was no Mr Kynaston, no Cyril Hawkin now by whom she could be admired, or with whom she could make music. She spent a lot of time playing the piano, sometimes made up little tunes, little songs, but then who would be interested now?

"I don't want you, stick in the mud, stick in the mud, I don't want you stick in the mud," she crooned to one of her little invented tunes. She had no job, she missed being a Red Cross commandant. She felt too young to retire into the role of an over-critical old grandmother. True she enjoyed baby-sitting for her grandchildren; true she enjoyed playing duets with her son-in-law Peter on the piano - the baby grand Ned had recently bought for her. She still went to some WI meetings, but not so often now, since the fun she had with those pantomimes, and wartime plays and sketches, was no longer a feasible outlet for her pent up energy. She wanted to dance, to sing, to act, to enjoy moments of complete involvement again.

She found her relaxation at last with the inmates of an old-style workhouse, a large stranded building in the middle of the countryside. The inmates were friendly and unpretentious, even if they were locked away from the world and labelled mentally abnormal. These were people with whom she could dance to the rhythm of old gramophone records, laugh at infantile jokes, relax, feel unrestricted by the conventions of life, be as mad as she felt like being. With such simple people she could take delight in simple pleasures - she could in some curious way feel at home with them all. There was the added attraction that she knew how much the forlorn and stranded inmates looked forward to her visits, and enjoyed them as much as she did. She understood now how Aunt Penelope must once have felt. One could escape into madness, into the refuge of one's unrestricted self.

When she was young she always wanted to be ordinary, to fit into the conventions of life, to do what other girls did - stay at home when she was small, go to school when she was older, go to university perhaps. But strange things always seemed to happen to her, to make her stand out as someone different from the crowd. It had been her own fault sometimes, she couldn't deny that. It wasn't until she was married and started her family that she had felt at last she started to fit into the ordinary world. She had her children christened, confirmed, sent to public schools, she hadn't wanted them to feel different.

There had been all those experiences - visions - dreams - whatever you liked to call them, that neither she nor anyone else seemed able to explain. Men, with all their scientific ideas found it hard to understand anything that didn't fit in with their factual way of looking at the world.

She suspected now, as she enjoyed the company of her friends, that it was the conventions of the world which were strange, that the hidden things of the mind - the part of living that was mostly ignored by what was called the civilised world - were the true reality. Intuition, the meeting of minds, seeing into the future, telepathy, those were things that should really be thought of as ordinary. Perhaps all the time she had been the one who was ordinary, while the mad world of science and convention was rushing the world into destruction. Men should listen more to women, to those things that men dismissed because they couldn't understand them. Men should use the other side of their brain.

She had seen the look Ruth gave her sometimes, others too,

as if she was finding it difficult to fit into the patterns of behaviour that were expected of her. If she wanted to wander round the village in the middle of the night, for example, why shouldn't she? They can think what they like, she thought, perhaps one day they will discover for themselves what is truly important.

Chapter 30
The End Result

Another day, another taxi ride to the hospital. Ned was sitting up in bed, or rather he was propped up by all his pillows, as if he could no longer support himself. How thin his face looked. She thought at first he was asleep, but he turned his head towards her. She had a letter from Canada, and asked if he would like her to read it to him. Almost imperceptibly, he shook his head. He opened his eyes and looked at her.

"We managed it between us, didn't we?" he said in a slow whisper, but with almost the old twinkle in his eyes, "You and I, we can say we created a whole tribe between us." Then a pause, his attention seemed to be drifting away again. Mollie watched with apprehension.

"Even started a new colony in Canada," he murmured.

"They send their love," she said.

"We had fun, didn't we?" he whispered.

The nurse came in to give him some kind of medicine. The effort of swallowing it seemed almost too much for him.

"I wouldn't stay too long," she said, "you can see how very tired he is."

She stood up to go. Ned lifted his hand, she bent down to hear what he was saying.

"It's been arranged," he said, "tomorrow morning...." and his voice trailed off. Asleep again she thought. That medicine he was given, no wonder he was so sleepy.

As she left, she wondered if perhaps those were the last words she would ever hear him say.

Ruth came to take her home.

"I've spoken to the nurse" she said. "There's nothing else that can be done for him. Just a matter of time. Would you like someone to spend the night with you at Strangers Corner? The nurse will ring me if there's any change." Mollie shook her head, she would rather be alone. Some time next morning she made herself a cup of coffee. She had been up for hours - without sleep a bed could feel very uncomfortable. She had been wandering round the garden looking at the plants that Ned had ordered, the grass he had no longer been able to cut, the gate he tried to repair. Her feet were wet, she was tired, she needed to sit down. She lowered herself gratefully into her chair, and lighted yet another cigarette. The ashtray was full by now of discarded cigarette butts.

There was a knock on the door, which for several minutes she ignored. It was hard to focus attention on the present.

"Come in," she said, irritably. The family didn't usually knock, just walked in, perhaps they were being especially considerate this morning. Then she remembered vaguely what Ned had said - something about tomorrow morning - but what about this morning?

The door opened and a man stood there in the shadow of the doorway.

She had no need to ask - she knew - straightaway she knew - who it was standing there. He was peering doubtfully into the room, as if he was not sure he had come to the right place, disconcerted by the fact that the door opened directly into the sitting room.

"Mollie?" he said inquiringly. She nodded. He walked in and held out his hand. It seemed such a strange formal encounter after all those years and years of separation and her longing for just such a meeting. All that time imagining what he might look like, what his life had been like. She got to her feet and took his proffered hand, and then almost withdrew it again, as a strange sensation travelled up her arm, like a mild electric shock. So unexpected. He felt the same, she could see it in his eyes.

"I think you are my mother, my natural mother," he explained. They stood there looking at each other, looking for points of recognition, she supposed, summing each other up. He was older than she had imagined him, but then by now he would be - she tried to calculate exactly but gave it up - he would be about seventy by now she concluded. He was prosperous-looking, slim, not too tall, with blue eyes and short grey hair. She thought she could see something familiar in his face - a fleeting expression she half recognised. Was it the set of his eyes, the way he smiled, the way he gestured with his hands, the way he stood? He was someone she didn't know, but half recognised for all that.

What did he make of her, she wondered, as they stood taking in each other's appearance. She wished he could have seen her when she was younger, when her hair was not grey, before she had become so thin, before she had grown to look so stooped and old, when she could still play the piano - did he play the piano, she wondered, did he like music?

How had he got here? The Masons must have very good connections to have found out about someone who vanished so completely all those years ago. Bewildered, happy, sad, elated, emotions chased each other through her mind.

"Sit down, won't you?" she said feeling awkwardly formal again, yet not knowing quite how else to proceed. She could have flung her arms round him, but then that might have startled him, made him feel uncomfortable. What claim had she on him, why should he be interested? Why had he come? But she couldn't but be grateful.

"How did you find me?" she asked. A silly question, it was she who had been doing the searching - not him. Ned said the Masons had been searching on her behalf, because Ned knew how in recent years she had so longed to meet him at last. "Just to see what he's like, if nothing else," she had said.

They sat facing each other.

"My name is Edward," he announced, "and may I call you Mollie? Anything more formal at our age would seem unnecessary, don't you think, pedantic even. Mollie is the name by which my father refers to my mother in his papers. I've done my best to make sure you are who I think you are - that is my natural mother."

He spoke in a rush, embarrassed perhaps, uncertain of his ground.

Mollie was still finding it difficult to get her bearings in this extraordinary encounter.

"I would have hesitated to make contact with you, you know, after all these years, if I hadn't thought that you were as anxious as

I am that we should meet." Mollie merely nodded in acquiescence.

"Do you believe in fate?" he asked, "or do you think it was telepathy - both of us trying to contact each other like that at the same time? There's no other way we could possibly have found one another except through a coincidence like that."

"Telepathy perhaps," Mollie said, "I've always wondered how it is that people can communicate with each other at a distance. It just happens sometimes. Scientists laugh at the idea, I know, but they don't know as much as they think they do."

"I've had the same kind of experience myself. I've certainly thought a lot about you recently."

Mollie looked at him inquiringly.

"Let me explain about my father - rather the man I always regarded as my father until he died a few months ago. He had been ill for many many years, the result of a Second World War injury. You must understand that since then he had been confused, he didn't realise much of what was going on around him, he could no longer conduct his own affairs."

"Would you like a cup of coffee?" Mollie asked unexpectedly. She was embarrassed sitting there with a cup in her hand, as he continued to talk.

"Let me get it" he said, and he went into the kitchen and helped himself. He came and sat down in front of her again.

"My mother" - he corrected himself - "the woman I always thought of as my mother - died when I was quite young. I was mostly brought up by an aunt."

"I never had reason to doubt my parentage, never had reason to look much into the past. I had my own life to lead, I got married, had children to bring up, and then my helpless father to care for, the estates to run."

She looked at him more carefully. Yes, she could see he was the kind of person you could rely on, someone used to giving orders - prosperous - self-confident.

"When my father died he left some papers, which had been locked up in a bank deposit box for many years. I certainly didn't know anything about them until recently. I've been trying ever since to read them to sort things out."

He brushed the hair back from his forehead. It was quite a shock as she recalled that Tom had been apt to do exactly the same thing.

"You can imagine my confusion, the strange feelings I had when I discovered I was not my father's son, nor for that matter was my mother my real mother. It was all to do with the time they both spent in Belgium. It must have been somewhere around 1906, for that's when I am told I was born. He was working for a company in Mons. What the papers explain is that my mother seemed unable to have children. She was never very strong, and when the opportunity arose to adopt a baby while they were abroad, it seemed too good an opportunity to miss. They came home proclaiming my mother had given birth to me while they had been away."

"What was she like, your mother?" Mollie often tried to imagine the woman who had looked after her baby.

"I don't remember very well, I was quite young when she died, but I do have a picture of her. I thought you might be interested to see some photographs, so I brought some along with me."

But the photograph meant nothing now to Mollie, it might have been of anyone. She had a smiling, kindly face. She had probably been a good mother to him while she was alive.

She was more interested in the photographs of his wife, but most of all his children, her 'other' grandchildren - two girls and two boys - laughing good-looking children.

"But let me continue. Alan Hutchinson, whom the Masons said you were enquiring after, was my father's friend, and my godfather. He played a considerable part in the arrangements that were made after I was born. I remember him so well, my dear Uncle Alan who brought me presents, took me out, was always there when I needed someone to talk to. He was like a second father to me." Edward seemed lost in thought for a few minutes.

"He was killed during the war, the Second World War, that is, did you know that?" he said sadly. "Killed by a bomb in London somewhere, I've been told."

"I met him several times," Mollie said, "I'd some vague idea he was connected with my past, there was something familiar about him, but I never could make out what the connection might have been."

"It was Alan who made all the arrangements for you in Belgium," Edward continued, "made sure you had a midwife, and took me to the foundling hospital afterwards. It was important that as a baby I could never be traced back to you, as you can understand. Alan, and my father too to give him his due, felt some responsibility towards you. As I understand it, he swore Alan to strict secrecy over the deception, since a considerable inheritance was at stake. If it had become known I was adopted there would have been all kinds of legal problems to contend with."

"I can quite understand that," Mollie said, "it never does to let your affairs get into the hands of lawyers."

"You sound as if you speak from some bad personal experience," he said, slightly amused at her forthrightness, "but of course you're right, that's just what my father said, never trust a lawyer. But to continue - my father provided money for you to stay at the convent in Mons so you could finish your education. He keeps saying in his letters that he thinks you were far too nice a girl, far too young, to have been wandering about Belgium with a concert band. He thought someone should take some responsibility for your welfare. One of the nuns at the convent was Alan's sister - Veronica she was called. You must have known her quite well I expect. I don't suppose you'd any idea she had a brother."

"I met your father, I think it must have been him," Mollie said, "when I was in Austria with my aunt. It always puzzled me as to who the man who was with him might be, and I've often wondered how Mr Hutchinson could have known where to find me. He spoke to me by name, you know."

"Your friend Grace, that's how. She was always writing to Veronica, and somehow many of the letters ended up in my father's possession. She and Alan must always have known what you were doing through those letters. I know my father, my adoptive father - met you once, a letter says so. It seems strange to think my father once met you all those years ago, while you were in Austria. In the cathedral wasn't it? He insisted he wanted to meet you, just once, to meet the girl who was his son's natural mother."

"He was very aristocratic looking I remember that. I've always imagined he was a Lord or something."

"The least said about my adoptive family the better I think, but what was my natural father like?"

"Amusing, attractive, and very musical. You have one of his gestures, the way you push your hair up on you forehead." To Mollie's amusement he put his hand up to his head, testing his mannerism.

"Is that all you remember? You haven't got a picture or anything?" Mollie shook her head.

"What a rotter he must have been, dumping you like that, he should have married you, taken care of you and the baby."

"It wasn't all his fault. He was married already you see, although he never told me until he knew I was pregnant. He hadn't seen his wife for years. Besides, he had problems of his own. He had no money, was in debt. He thought I would be safe at the convent, properly looked after. He died quite soon after you know, he knew how ill he was. But all that is so long ago. You were a love child, isn't that what they say? Tom gave me two of the happiest years of my life. I don't blame him for anything."

There was a pause. Mollie was feeling exhausted. So much information to take in, so much emotion to contend with. She shivered, it was cold today.

Edward picked up the rug from the back of the chair and wrapped it round her as she sat there. He kissed her on the cheek, a gentle kiss that almost made her cry.

"Goodbye mother," he said. "I'm so glad to have met you. We are much alike, you know, you and I." And he was gone.

Was it minutes, hours, days later that Ruth was gently shaking her? Had she been dreaming or had someone called Edward - who claimed to be her son - actually been here in this room with her. Dream or no dream she could think about him now - know what kind of a person he had become - what her other grandchildren looked like - know that his life had been a happy and prosperous one. That she had been right to give away her baby all those years ago.

Ruth was still shaking her.

"Who was that man that just left - went off in a car?"

"Something to do with the Masons, that's all" she answered.

"They've rung from the hospital," Ruth said.